Three Papers of W.R. Bion

Three Papers of W.R. Bion features two previously unpublished papers and one which has only previously appeared in *The Complete Works of W. R. Bion* (2014). Characterised by Bion's directness, clarity and intensity, they illustrate important aspects of his later thinking. They also see Bion using his key ideas in fresh contexts which will allow readers already familiar with his theoretical and clinical concepts to appreciate them from a new angle.

The first paper, *Memory and Desire*, clarifies one of Bion's most important and clinically-relevant ideas: the value of suspending elements of our memory and desire in the service of allowing openness to psychoanalytic intuition. The second, *Negative Capability*, was reformulated to become the final chapter of his 1970 *Attention and Interpretation*. The publication here of the original paper allows an interesting and rewarding three-way comparison to be made with the 1970 chapter, and *Memory and Desire*. The third paper, *Break Up, Break Down, Break Through*, was presented without notes in 1976 in Los Angeles and the transcript from the recorded talk is published here for the first time. It displays the complex interweaving of the personal and the theoretical and offers a fascinating contribution to the study of what Bion called "the turbulence that obeys no man-made 'laws of nature'".

Wilfred R. Bion's writing continues to be read and re-read by an increasing and widening readership; the three papers presented here possess contemporary clinical relevance and each have a bearing on the underlying philosophical basis of psychoanalytical work and thinking.

Chris Mawson is a training and supervising analyst of the British Psychoanalytical Society and works in private practice as a psychoanalyst. He is Editor of *The Complete Works of W. R. Bion* (2014), alongside Consulting Editor Francesca Bion.

Three Papers of W.R. Bion

Edited by Chris Mawson

Routledge
Taylor & Francis Group
LONDON AND NEW YORK

First published 2018
by Routledge
2 Park Square, Milton Park, Abingdon, Oxon OX14 4RN

and by Routledge
711 Third Avenue, New York, NY 10017

Routledge is an imprint of the Taylor & Francis Group, an informa business

British Library Cataloguing in Publication Data
A catalogue record for this book is available from the British Library

Library of Congress Cataloging in Publication Data
A catalog record for this book has been requested

ISBN: 978-1-138-61499-4 (hbk)
ISBN: 978-1-138-61505-2 (pbk)
ISBN: 978-0-429-45455-4 (ebk)

Typeset in Times New Roman
by Taylor & Francis Books

Contents

Even the individual person hates housing or developing a new idea, because if you do, it is inevitable that you feel you should have got it right the last time. The inevitable discovery that you have been mistaken is a dreadful thing to discover. It also carries with it the feeling that if your own ideas change, then all the problems that you have ever solved are re-opened because they have a relationship of things-not-oneself with oneself. You can appreciate how confusing this gets.

W. R. Bion, *Break Up, Break Through, Break Down* (1975)

Foreword

Ronald Britton

I think the publication of these three papers is of considerable importance to serious scholars of Wilfred Bion's writings, happily a growing number, and also to a larger group, that is of those interested and influenced, maybe even unknowingly, by his ideas in their own clinical work. Some of the phrases have become very familiar, such as negative capability, container and contained or selected fact, but to rescue them from the risk of becoming half-understood clichés and to really understand what they are about we need to see them in context. This, thanks to Chris Mawson's impressive editorship of *The Complete Works of W. R. Bion,* is now more possible and I am glad he has decided to add to that these three papers, of which two are previously unpublished and one appears so far only in *The Complete Works.* In the first two, based on recordings of papers at Scientific Meetings, we get the feeling of what it was like to hear Bion at a point when he was seeking to persuade his colleagues to join him in a new enterprise – an endeavour to purify clinical practice to more accurately represent the transactions of psychoanalysis and to disencumber them from over valued theories and archaic presuppositions. Bion was clearly convinced that psychoanalytic practice was a means of exploring the human mind and he was keen to do so in the context of new twentieth-century natural science with its philosophical implications.

His new project, which I think began in 1959, was to do this in the light of fundamental changes in the most basic of the natural sciences, physics. Freud had wished to base his theorising on physics from the beginning of psychoanalysis but the science he knew then was classical Newtonian physics. As in post-Chomsky brain-based linguistics, universal grammar is, as Steven Pinker suggested, based on physics, but it is the wrong physics. Our brain-based minds have evolved on our small planet with its relatively slow movements. But thanks to our newly developed ability to penetrate the atom and survey the cosmos our understanding of material reality has been transformed, particularly by the mathematical inspirations of the quantum scientists and Einstein's theory of relativity. Bion had become aware of this and wanted to align psychoanalysis with the new scientific approaches.

Heisenberg lucidly explains his own conceptual discovery of the 'uncertainty principle' and demonstrates that classical logic is superseded by quantum logic in the scientific, mathematical comprehension of the material world. In everyday life, he says, classical logic is adequate, but not sub-atomically and not cosmically. Heisenberg wrote this in 1958. Now we live daily in a world where the transistors in our computers and mobiles, and our familiar lasers are based on quantum physics, and the satnav in our cars is adjusted daily according to Einstein' s theory of relativity. I doubt if the use of machinery based on such revolutionary physics has displaced our natural beliefs about the world we live in.

Bion was reading Braithwaite's *Scientific Explanation: A Study of the Function of Theory, Probability and Law in Science* in 1959, at the time he was writing *Attacks on Linking*, but it is in his subsequent books, starting with *Learning from Experience* in 1962, that Braithwaite's influence is most evident. Bion's comment on reading Braithwaite says a great deal about his developing rigour in accounts of analytic experience:

> I cannot help thinking as I read this book …what a terrible lot of bilge I have read in my time. There has always been a certain amount, too much I think, of gullibility about me, and it makes me swallow a lot of nonsense …I wish I could feel more confident that I wouldn't add to the flood of rot but of course if I did I would probably lack the necessary self-criticism.
>
> Bion, 1985, pp. 123–4

What Bion took from Braithwaite was his idea that a scientific theory is a general deductive system which has particular observable consequences, and which can only be seen in practice. The SDS (Scientific Deductive System) itself should be in the form of a mathematical calculus. The measurable consequences of the generality can be verified only in particular examples; they can negate the SDS by being contrary to expectation but they can never prove it. The SDS provides a means of working with these abstractions as formulae without needing particulars to illustrate them, as in the mathematics of theoretical physics. One can see how Bion, constantly thinking about how to relate particular experience to general hypotheses, is drawn to Braithwaite. It inspired his creation of the 'Grid'. In this he ingeniously turns it upside down so that the basic data comes first, to be followed by its organization into a model which in turn in some unrealizable time would become a Scientific Deductive System. This is the heart of Braithwaite's exposition of scientific conceptualisation.

> As the hypotheses of increasing generality rises, the concepts with which the hypotheses are concerned cease to be the properties of hints which are directly observable and instead become 'theoretical' concepts – atoms, electron, fields of force, genes, unconscious mental processes – which are connected to the observable facts by complicated logical relationships.
>
> Braithwaite, 1968, p. ix

His reading of Braithwaite in 1958 crystallized Bion's attempt to encourage psychoanalysts to move their theorising upwards from their observation of empirical events through a classifiable phenomenology to a definitory scientific hypothesis (SDS), which is a general proposition that convers all the things of a certain sort.

Bion could take heart however from reading Poincaré, who pointed out that science does not start from *all* the facts, which are multitudinous, but from intuitively selected facts which like nuclei form webs of already known old facts and new ones. I would now use the term model to describe these articulated belief systems.

Bion, reading Heisenberg, grasped that certainty had been replaced at the heart of physical science by probability: that is that the electron does not move on a pre-determined path with the certainty that it would turn up in a predictable place but that there was a very high degree of probability that it would. Bion also saw a parallel between theoretical physics and psychoanalytic theory, commenting that a theory was a hypothesis about a hypothesis about a hypothesis. This is a paraphrase of Heisenberg, who wrote of different levels of language,

> one level refers to the objects for instance atoms or electrons. A second level refers to statements about statements about objects. A third level may refer to statements about statements about objects etc.
>
> Heisenberg, 1958, p. 125

Probably the most disturbing of Heisenberg's ideas, for Bion then and for us now, concerns the overthrow of classical logic exemplified in Newton's physics. In classical logic if a thing (a) is here and not there, then the statement 'it is true that a is here' is equal to the statement 'it is not true that a is not here'. In quantum logic this is not the case; in mathematical terms these statements do not compute (that is a+b does not equal b+a). The electron can be a bit here and a bit there because it is only potential, and does not really exist until it interacts with something. What Quantum thinking has moved us forward to is a realization that what the physical world is composed of is interactions not bits of matter. This is all very well in the quantum mathematical universe or the sub-atomic laboratories such as the Hadron collider, but we do not, and probably cannot, think like that in our daily life.

This takes us, as it did Bion, back to David Hume's seventeenth century, philosophical, *Enquiry Concerning Human Understanding*. Bion takes from Hume the notion of 'constantly conjoined' phenomena, which he substituted for the presumptive notion of 'cause and effect'. Hume's rigorous logic was thought by a number of philosophers to negate science, but it has been vindicated by twentieth century physics. But Hume also realized that living in this logically rigorous, stripped down, conceptually abstinent mental world was emotionally impossible. So he happily regained his natural, unjustified, beliefs when he re-joined his friends socially. Hume's philosophical study, where rigorous reasoning is practiced uncorrupted by hidden assumptions or older values, has some resemblance to the psychoanalytic consulting room Bion advocated in these papers.

The determination that followed from this excursion into scientific method, or what we could call scientific practice, is what led to the papers in this book. For Bion, psychoanalytic practice is what his mentor Wilfred Trotter, the famous Surgeon and author of *Instincts of the Herd in Peace and War*, called a practical art; a term he used for medicine and other professions such as law, architecture, farming or carpentry: skilful activities where learning procedure and apprenticeship is involved. The interplay between practice and theory is one of Bion's preoccupations. Ultimately he agrees with Braithwaite and Heisenberg: it is science if it accommodates empirical observation, even if – as in quantum physics – the theoretical (mathematical) development is hugely original and elaborate and confirmation may be along time coming. The physicists would be the first to agree that it begins and ends with empirical observation and is always susceptible to empirical findings. In psychoanalysis, as Bion asserts, we move from D (security) to Ps (patience) and back again. I would prefer to call it D (conviction) to PS (uncertainty) in a sequence of Ps(n) to D(n) to PS(n+1) to D(n+1)… each step including more information. Knowledge develops through epistemic crises, D to PS, which Bion called catastrophic change, the title of another paper given at a Scientific meeting in 1966.

The third of these papers is written a decade later and is quite different in tone. This tone resembles that of one of Freud's last papers,

Analysis Terminable and Interminable. It is retrospective, unillusioned but not disillusioned, pessimistic, but imaginatively speculative.

It is however encouraging to we practitioners, having been exhorted to relinquish fondly held theories and any aspiration to cure, to find Bion observing in his 1965 *Memory and Desire* paper that:

> When it comes to the actual progress of the analysis, I have found that it is very extraordinary – the way in which the experience, as it evolves in the analytic situation, is, over and over again, recognizable. That over and over again the ordinary theories of analysis – whatever your school may be, whatever your private bent of mind may be, and the theories that you may hold – how much easier it becomes to be able to appreciate that what is happening in the consulting room is an actual approximation to one or other of the theories that you know, no matter how little you may feel that you know about psychoanalysis or psychoanalytic theories. It is extraordinary how much one does know, and how often the theories that have already been discovered which are a commonplace of psychoanalytic literature, swim into view, so to speak, irresistibly, because of what is happening in the consulting room.

It is extraordinary in other words how true many of the accumulation of psychoanalytic theories turn out to be. This many of us can vouch for and it is almost a paraphrase of what Heisenberg wrote about physics. It is that which in times of 'catastrophic change' gives faith to analysts and scientists alike. Faith says it may not make psychoanalytic sense here and now but somewhere, someday it will, as it has in the past.

Introduction

Chris Mawson

Of the three papers in this volume, two have never been published before, and one appears only in *The Complete Works of W. R. Bion* (2014). Each of the papers is characterised by Bion's directness, clarity and intensity, and reflects important aspects of Bion's later thinking. Where they appear to contain previously well-worked ideas they do so in fresh contexts which allow readers already familiar with his theoretical and clinical concepts to appreciate them from a new angle, and perhaps in some cases to match them with their own experiences.

The first paper, *Memory and Desire*, was transcribed by the editor from Bion's spoken version which he presented without notes at a Scientific Meeting of the British Psychoanalytical Society on Wednesday 16 June 1965. A significant contribution to clarifying one of his most important and clinically relevant ideas, it is a more accessible and less condensed account than his two-page *Notes on Memory and Desire*, first published in *Psychoanalytic Forum* in the autumn of 1967.

Bion often prefaced his presentations with an apology for not having circulated them in the form of a written paper. In fact he preferred not to do so, and although in some cases he had prepared for a talk by speaking his ideas into a tape recorder, his presentation of his ideas was without notes and very often a written paper was not forthcoming at all. When one eventually appeared, it usually did not bear a close relationship with his spoken version. The second paper in this volume, *Negative Capability*, was reformulated to become the final chapter of his 1970 book, *Attention and Interpretation: A Scientific Approach To Insight In Psycho-Analysis and Groups,* with the title: *Prelude to or Substitute for Achievement.* The publication here of *Negative Capability* allows an interesting and rewarding three-way comparison to be made with that 1970 version, and with the 1965 *Memory and Desire* paper at the beginning of this collection.

The third paper, *Break Up, Break Down, Break Through*, was presented without notes on 9 December 1976, to members of The Study Centre for Organizational Leadership and Authority (SCOLA) in Los Angeles. In the preparation of Bion's complete works the rough transcript of the recorded talk looked unpromising in terms of its suitability for publication, and in consultation with Francesca Bion the decision was taken not to include it in the Complete Works. At the time it was felt by both of us that it would require too much speculative editing work. A decade further on, however, it seemed a good idea to reconsider this paper, both in the light of the accumulated experience of editing the entirety of his published and unpublished work, and also because of what I came to see as the importance of the complex interweaving in it of the personal and the theoretical. Many analysts had come to believe that the paper had been written, and some even wrote of its existence. On 16 July 1977 in Italy Bion said the following:

> The emotional turbulence which is initiated is of some consequence because all sorts of elements, to which we don't usually pay much attention and of which we are not aware, get churned up and thrown onto the surface. They are often so noticeable that we give them a name – I tried to summarize it in a talk called "Break Up, Break Down, Break Through".

This quotation is a beautifully concise summary of the *Break Up, Break Down, Break Through* paper. Emotional turbulence is one of Bion's most important themes. In *The Memoir of the Future* (1977, II, p. 1) he called it, "the turbulence that obeys no man-made 'laws of nature'", and this third paper in the collection is a fascinating contribution to the study of it.

Paper I

Memory and Desire[1]

W. R. Bion 1965

What I want to do this evening is something which is rather different from a scientific paper; it is a discussion of the subject in which I am interested, and I hope that it will interest you. The first point I would make is this: It is a paper about an event that hasn't taken place yet. The remarks I am making are addressed specifically to analysts who are seeing a patient tomorrow, or the day after. I think it would be helpful to focus not so much on what I am saying as on tomorrow's session; the one you are going to have tomorrow with the particular patient.

Now, to turn to the title of the paper: These two terms – Memory and Desire – I intend to use as what I have called elsewhere 'terms which bind a constant conjunction'. By a constant conjunction I mean that in certain circumstances you might notice that certain elements kept on turning up constantly conjoined; that you think, for example, that there is fur, claws, whiskers – and you bind the lot by saying "Cat"; the object of that being that once you have bound this constant conjunction you can then set about researching, as superficially or as deeply as you choose, into what you mean by this term. It is rather different from the ordinary view – about the ordinary views which are held philosophically about abstraction. I am really suggesting that you start with the unknown, that you note a constant conjunction, that you bind it by a term which is virtually meaningless, and then proceed to investigate what you mean by that term, for the rest of your life if you are so inclined.

The first term, Memory: the constant conjunction which I wish to bind by that is very much, probably, what we all understand by that term in ordinary conversation. One might say that it also includes the ideas which Freud expresses when he speaks of Notation and of its relation to memory in the paper on the two principles of mental functioning.[2]

It is also related to what we ordinarily mean when we talk about cases that we have seen, in scientific papers and elsewhere, and describe what we consider to be accounts of what took place. It is probably also the kind of thing that we try, at various times in our careers, to make notes about – so that we shall be able to know, or to remember, what has taken place in sessions, and then be able to report on them and to refer to these notes and so on. That, roughly speaking, is what I mean by the use of the term memory.

Similarly with regard to desire – again it is a meaning which most of us are aware of in our ordinary conversation – I mean by it something rather positively covetous, as it were; something that one wants to have. It has a certain similarity to memory, in that one could say about memory that you tend to remember various things which you like to possess and in this sense memory itself is very often used as if it were a container, in which one keeps these objects which one desires.

I also want to include in the term Desire something which Freud speaks of as wish-fulfilment, and the expression of wishes in dreams; it is similar to that. When we go into this matter further, and I am talking now specifically of the way in which I use these terms (all of this is by way of being a definition of what I am trying to talk about), the elements about which I am concerned are, really, sensuous images; that is, both desires and memories are spoken of in terms which are derived from a background of sensuous experience. Let's say that here are things which you can touch, or feel, or smell, which are felt to have a shape or a form, and so on. The fact that they are expressed and stored in terms of this kind also means that they are very closely related to the primitive background of senses, and very frequently to a phase in development in which the pleasure-pain principle is dominant. The consequence is that the terms in which these things are remembered or in which they are desired are suitable to objects which can be sensuously perceived and which can be regarded as painful or pleasant. Therefore the *scope* is relatively limited.

Now, I am aware that this is not the only meaning of memory. I am trying all the time to put a limit onto it, so it should apply to what I want to talk about, but for the sake of completeness I think that it is well for us to pay attention to the fact that one could say that even a mathematical formula can be used as a method by which you express or store a memory. I don't think, however, that when it comes to clinical work – when it comes to this session tomorrow – when one thinks of memory, that one is going to think of it in mathematical terms or anything like it. The terms will almost certainly be of this primitive kind, suitable for expressing sensuous experience; suitable for expressing experiences which are felt to be related either to pain or to pleasure.

The other elements, which I want to touch on briefly, I have thought of in terms of the Grid which I drew up, in which one axis states, as it were, the genetic phase of a particular element that one is trying to categorise, and on the other hand, the horizontal axis, which expresses the use to which it is put. It is quite obvious that there can be highly developed formulations: thoughts, theories, ideas, even mathematical formulations as I have said, which can be used in a highly sophisticated way; I am not concerning myself with that, for the reasons I have already given – because what I am concerned with are the terms in which we usually think about our cases.

At this point perhaps I ought to make clear that I have always been sceptical about what are called 'clinical accounts'. I have felt that they are, after all, only versions of what took place: they are transformations of what was a real experience. Most of us are critical, for various reasons, of a clinical description. I have felt increasingly disinclined even to pretend to give a clinical account of what takes place because even if one is simply concerned with simplifying the events of a complicated situation, the distortion is really terrific. Nevertheless, as analysts we do know – and I think it is borne in on us more and more as experience builds up – that we really do deal with *something*; that the psychoanalytic experience, however sceptical we may be, is really an emotional experience and it really exists, even if we shall never know or shall be in a position to give even an approximately correct description of what takes place. For this reason I find it most useful to think of any clinical description as being by nature of a pictorial representation, or shall we say a sensuous representation (because I am thinking of what takes place in an analytic situation) – I transform that situation into visual images and then a further transformation into verbal formulations, such as those with which we are familiar here. These transformations are of a kind in which one gets an increasing degree of sophistication, but the most comprehensible – the most easy to grasp – and therefore the reason why one frequently is asked, 'Can you give an example?'; 'can you illustrate this?'; 'can you give me a clinical account which matches this?'; it is because it is much easier to be able to grasp either a visual presentation or a verbalisation of that visual presentation.

Now, while there is a gain in communicability of such a formulation, there is a loss of accuracy – for the reasons that I have given: one is using terms which come from a sensuous background to describe this, and there are other reasons with which I am not bothering tonight, but which are known to all of us through the experience of our own analysis.

My point is that this reality which we all know about, which we feel is unmistakeably borne-in on us in the course of analytic work, is then something which cannot really be properly expressed, because if you take, shall we say, an anxiety state, most of us would expect to be able to recognize anxiety when we meet it,[3] but you can't smell it; it hasn't got a shape; you can't touch it; and so on. And by the time you *can* represent what is going on – in the terms which we ordinarily use – a very considerable development has taken place. The event itself – the thing itself, anxiety itself – has been transformed in a very striking way, by the time you use a word like 'anxiety'.

This brings me to the point that any verbal description, any notes that we may make, practically any formulations are, really, distortions. I am not talking now about pathological states. I am not talking about this subject as it occurs looked at from the point of view of psychopathology, or from the point of view of the patient. I am considering it simply from the point of view of each one of us who has a patient to see tomorrow. Therefore I am not concerning myself with either of these questions as being psychopathological manifestations, because on this I think that we all are in general agreement: it is considered to be absolutely essential, at least in our society, that people should be analysed, and that we do not know of any better way of looking after this problem than by insisting that people should be analysed in order to deal with it.

What I am concerned with here is something much more conscious and under conscious control. I am not concerned with the problem of what one should do in order to be ready for, and in condition for, the session tomorrow.

It is well known, in other realms, that it is possible to be in training. To take a trivial example: if someone is playing squash, or tennis, it is not felt to be advisable that they should play static ball games such as golf. Similarly, I am suggesting that there should be a consideration besides this matter of psychopathology – the matters dealt with by analysis and so forth – of what is the desirable state of affairs if you are a psychoanalyst and you have got a patient to see tomorrow. What can be done in the way of keeping in training?

Now, I want to remind you of the conventional view which crops up, where there is a tendency to feel that it is important to remember what takes place in an analysis; that it is important to find some method by which you record it – to write notes or use a recording machine and so forth – and, the more critical the situation becomes, the more cause you have for anxiety about any patient, the more important it is felt to be to be able to remember what took place today in that patient's analysis, what took place yesterday, and so on.

The view that I am wanting to put is that this view is entirely mistaken. And not only mistaken, but positively bad for your analytic work. With regard to desire, I want to include things like thinking, 'How nice it will be when the session is over'; or 'How nice it will be when the Summer comes' – all ideas ideas of that kind, including – and this is an important point – 'How nice it would be to cure the patient'.

As you know, there is a great deal of discussion as to what the aim of analysis is. I think that in fact it is a mistaken preoccupation, although a very interesting one, for an analyst *while he is analysing*. I think that the desire to cure the patient should have no place whatsoever in the consulting room. Whatever place that it has in the make-up of the analyst or in his philosophical life; because, in my opinion, nothing will throw your judgement out more than to be concerned with trying to remember what the patient or you yourself have said, or wanting to cure the patient, or to entertain any other desire. In my experience I find nearly always that the wish to remember what the patient said, or any desire to cure the patient, invariably seems to me to crop up in the situation, and in a formulation, which is intended to keep at bay and to keep out of mind certain other feelings.

The point is brought home by those extremely brilliant (one might almost say) psychoanalysts – the psychotic patient, who, when he is concerned to break the link between the analyst and himself, will do his best to stimulate the analyst to remember something – that you will get floods of evocative words – and do his best to stimulate in the analyst a desire – if only a desire to get rid of him. This is because the stimulation of either of those two will virtually destroy the analyst's judgement. If the patient is successful in his aim your judgement disappears. Therefore – harking back to tomorrow's session – what I would like to say is that you should spend your time banishing any memory of the patient whatsoever, in preparation for the session, and any aim or ambition as regard to his cure. I do not mean by this that forgetting is a good thing – that is just as bad as remembering. I think that it is something which is a positive discipline. It is a matter which you will find is extremely difficult, and you have only got to think of it for a moment to see how inherently improbable it is. But so long as we are as we are – human beings – we shall entertain desires and we shall have memory. The view that I want to put is that our difficulty as analysts is not that we have such bad memories, or that we are deficient in a desire to cure our patients, but on the contrary is the intrusively powerful nature of these memories which, as you will realise, is quite compatible with views which Freud himself put forward with regard to the prominence in analysis of memories.

What I am suggesting then is that an effort is required which is an actual discipline, difficult to achieve; it cannot simply be achieved simply by contenting yourself with the fact that you have forgotten – that is not good enough. It is a matter of trying to get out of the habit of remembering things, and trying to get out of the habit of desiring or wanting anything *while you are predominantly engaged on your work* – I am not expressing views about this as a philosophy of life or anything; it is simply an attempt to promulgate an actual rule – as if one could make rules for psychoanalytic training. This is the kind of rule that I would like to make. I would like to stress once more that it is very different from the view that we are all used to – the view that we fall back into very easily: the more critical the situation, the more we try to remember something or other, even if it is only an appropriate theory – the direct contrary of what I think is desirable.

The consequences of this, in so far as I can speak of them, in so far as I am acquainted with them myself, are peculiar. I do not know how far I can go in an attempt to describe them. But one of the things about it is that in order to see clearly one really needs to be pretty well blind: metaphorically and literally. It is really a sort of positive lack of anything in one's mind, if one can put it like that; that the darker the spot[4] that you wish to illuminate, the darker you have to be – you have to shut out all light in order to see it; and only in that way is it possible to get the conditions in which a real object, but one which is formless and not in any way appreciable to what we ordinarily regard as the senses, emerges, evolves, and becomes possible for us to be aware of.

If one can approximate to this situation then I think that after a time it really does seem as if it is much clearer, as if one quite felt quite unmistakeably that what one was witnessing was, for example, anxiety, or hostility, and so forth. I said that I didn't want to deal at all here with psychopathology, but just as an aside I would like to suggest that this view also perhaps gives an idea of what the infant or the child has to put up with in dealing with quite real things – real experiences – but which cannot be expressed beyond by saying, "I feel I've got a tummy ache". That is the kind of vocabulary, those are the sensuous terms which have to be employed in order to describe a thing which is in no way represented by that at all. There is a quite striking phrase in *Civilization and its Discontents* where Freud, having given a description – a sort of model of the mind – then says that the striking thing about this, the thing you can really learn from it, is the utter inadequacy of a pictorial representation to provide a model for the mind. This really sums up very well indeed what I am trying to say, namely the fact that we are dealing with things which are real enough, which are absolutely real, even from earliest infancy on, but which cannot be expressed except in the kind of vocabulary which is quite unfitted for it by its derivation and characteristics.

When it comes to the actual progress of the analysis, I have found that it is very extraordinary – the way in which the experience, as it evolves in the analytic situation, is, over and over again, recognizable. That over and over again the ordinary theories of analysis – whatever your school may be, whatever your private bent of mind may be, and the theories that you may hold – how much easier it becomes to be able to appreciate that what is happening in the consulting room is an actual approximation to one or other of the theories that you know, no matter how little you may feel that you know about psychoanalysis or psychoanalytic theories. It is extraordinary how much one does know, and how often the theories that have already been discovered which are a commonplace of psychoanalytic literature, swim into view, so to speak, irresistibly, because of what is happening in the consulting room. But the first, essential thing here, is to be able to get into the state of mind in which these things which are not open to sensuous apprehension are nevertheless possible to apprehend.

The order in which this happens, however, seems to be different. I would not want to try to explain in what way it is different, but certainly it seems to me that a change takes place; there *is* a coherence about it; there is a respect in which the totality of the analysis hangs together; there is a way in which the pieces of the jigsaw can be seen to have a configuration which bears a relationship to the whole – even when you do not know what the whole is, but the order in which those events appear seems to me to be different when one tries to do analysis in this way, rather than in other ways in which one is familiar.

A further point is that I think it is quite a frightening way of doing it. For one thing, the cultural background to which we belong is the sort of background where, if anything went wrong, and you found yourself in a Court of Law or a Coroner's Court, it would be assumed as a matter of course that you really know something about your patient; that you know that your patient is married, has four children, say, and so on. And indeed, one feels that that is something one ought to know about. Now this is the dilemma: if you know that, and if you remember that, then it may take you quite a long time to appreciate the fact that your patient is talking in a way which is quite appropriate to his not being married at all, nor having any children. And the knowledge, the memory, that he is married and has children will easily distort one's view and interfere with one's judgement of the situation in which the interpretations are appropriate to his being unmarried and having no children, while one is tending to wish to make interpretations which would make allowance for the other facts. That is a crude example, but it is, roughly speaking, one aspect of it. On the other hand, there is a feeling that if it emerged that you did not even know that your patient was a married man, how very odd this would look, and what a queer light it would cast on any view of your professional competence, in the cultural background in which you belong.

One cannot do analysis on those terms, but at the same time I think that one cannot really do analysis on terms in which one is unaware of the risks that one is running and of the price that one has to pay if one is going to do analysis properly. If I am right in saying that this is *a* way of doing analysis properly, then, at the same time, one is going to pay the price of this in anxiety. So there *is* an increase in anxiety; I do not think that one could say that it is an undesirable increase in anxiety; on the contrary I think, again, that it probably would mark the division between those who practise psychoanalysis and those who talk about it. If you are a psychoanalyst, if you are seeing a patient tomorrow, then you are seeing that patient in a particular emotional situation. Not only in the consulting room but in the cultural situation, the cultural background. Therefore it is important for the analyst to be both the analyst and also a member of the society, so that he is exposed to the emotional experiences and states of mind of the society to which he belongs. It is, however, as I say, somewhat disconcerting and, at first, not at all pleasing. Again, with regard to the patient the situation is different, because what one is concerned to do, amongst other things, is to be able to observe the operation of his memories and of his desires. I think that it makes it very much easier when one keeps out of one's own mind these particular elements of memory and desire, because then it becomes possible to be able to 'see' what is operating in the patient's mind, and what is actually going on in the analytic session.

I raised the point a little while back about the transformation. I would like to revert again to that for a moment. Perhaps I can express it best in this way: If you see a painting of a corn-field most of us in this particular culture would recognize it for what it was. That must mean that there is something which is invariant; that there is something about the actual corn-field and there is something about the piece of canvas with the paint disposed on its surface, which remains unaltered[5] and which makes recognition possible. Another example, as you know, is that if you wish to represent a circular pond you have to draw an ellipse; if you wish to represent a path with parallel borders you have to represent it with lines which meet at a point.

What we are witnessing in an analytic session I don't think can ever *be* the real experience; we don't know what that is, but what we do know is the experience by the time it has been transformed – by the patient – into various forms of verbal representation. There is no reason why it shouldn't be other representations except that analytically we usually conduct it in terms of verbal communication, but of course as child analysts know, there are other methods of communication as well. If one ever analyses somebody who is by nature a musician it isn't very long before you find yourself up against somebody who is opposed to your whole method of expression; that there is a feeling that if he were to be allowed to play the piano then he could say what he thinks, and considers that he is being restricted to a feeble sort of method of communication such as conversation. So in this way the number of transformations that we have to deal with are really very considerable. Again, when you are presented with a verbal account by a patient, one could make a parallel to this by saying that you might have to look at the painting – say Constable's *Hay Wain* – and you can regard that as being a record of a hay wain, that that's what it is, very simply: It is about a hay wain. Now that is not really good enough for the analyst, because if you stick to that then you stick to this state of affairs where you know *about* analysis, and you know *about* the patient – you know that the patient is married and so forth. But what you don't know is the patient. There has therefore to be a quite different transformation.

Now, this other transformation is, I think, of a different sort of category altogether. It is to do with the actual emotional reality of the situation with which we are dealing. Now when you get onto that, then I think you are in difficulties because you are using language which is suitable for talking *about* something, but that is not a language which is necessarily suitable for an experience in which something is happening, a dynamic emotional experience which is not open to sensuous observation.

The final point, then, that I want to make is that as a prelude to this state of affairs where you are actually having to deal with, to psychoanalyse – whatever that may mean – a state of mind, then these special steps have to be taken; and that they have to be steps of this nature, where the question of desires and the question of memory have to be dealt with as definite matters of discipline – the banishment of them from the mind.

Notes

1 Paper given without notes at a Scientific Meeting at the British Psychoanalytical Society on Wednesday 16th June 1965 [Ed.]. Copyright © 2014 by The Estate of W. R. Bion. Printed by the kind permission of Paterson Marsh Ltd and Francesca Bion.

2 Freud, S. (1911, p. 220). 'Formulation on the Two Principles of Mental Functioning'. SE XII: 213–226 [Ed.]. "Consciousness now learned to comprehend sensory qualities in addition to the qualities of pleasure and unpleasure which hitherto had alone been of interest to it. A special function was instituted which had periodically to search the external world, in order that its data might be familiar already if an urgent internal need should arise – the function of *attention*. Its activity meets the sense-impressions half way, instead of awaiting their appearance. At the same time, probably, a system of *notation* was introduced, whose task it was to lay down the results of this periodical activity of consciousness – a part of what we call *memory*" [Ed.].

3 In the original talk it is: "most of us would expect to be able to recognize anxiety when we saw it, but you can't smell it etc.": 'Saw' has been amended to 'meet' for reasons which will be evident. [Ed.].

4 Bion here is following Freud, who wrote in a letter to Lou Andreas-Salomé on May 13, 1924:
"I know that in writing I have to blind myself artificially in order to focus all the light on one dark spot, renouncing cohesion, harmony, rhetoric and everything which you call symbolic, frightened as I am by the experience that any such claim or expectation involves the danger of distorting the matter under investigation, even though it may embellish it. Then you come along and add what is missing, build upon it, putting what has been isolated back into its proper context. I cannot always follow you, for my eyes, adapted as they are to the dark, probably can't stand strong light or an extensive range of vision". He made this link to Freud's letter explicit in the discussion following the presentation of his 1967 *Notes on memory and desire.* [Ed.].

5 Bion's thinking on this point is close to what Bertrand Russell stated in his introduction to Wittgenstein's *Tractatus,* that the representation and the represented must exhibit the same 'logical manifold' (the term used by Russell) which 'cannot be itself represented since it has to be in common between the fact and the picture' [Ed.].

Editor's postscript

> Even the simple act which we describe as 'seeing someone we know' is, to some extent, an intellectual process. We pack the physical outline of the creature we see with all the ideas we already formed about him, and in the complete picture of him which we compose in our minds those ideas have certainly the principal place. In the end they come to fill out so completely the curve of his cheeks, to follow so exactly the line of his nose, they blend so harmoniously in the sound of his voice that these seem to be no more than a transparent envelope, so that each time we see the face or hear the voice it is our own ideas of him which we recognize and to which we listen.
>
> Marcel Proust, *Swann's Way: Remembrance of Things Past, Volume One*

Bion's original presentation of his ideas on Memory and Desire, given on the 16th June 1965 at a Scientific Meeting of the British Psycho-analytical Society, was not published at the time because he gave it without notes, apologizing to his audience at the beginning and undertaking to provide a written version at some point. He said that if he had written down what he wanted to say about the two terms of his paper, he felt it would have made little sense. In 1967 he published the bare bones of the paper as a two page article, *Notes on Memory and Desire*, first in *Psychoanalytic Forum* (1967, 2/3: 271–280). It was reprinted in 1988 in *Melanie Klein Today*, edited by Elizabeth Spillius, and was also appended at the end of Bion's 1995 book, *Cogitations.* When Bion presented the *Notes*, several analysts took part in the discussion of it but only Bion's responses were published.[1]

There are a great many references in Bion's work to the principles he articulated in such a condensed way in his brief, pithy *Notes on Memory and Desire.* There is an extended treatment of the ideas in his *Attention and Interpretation: A Scientific Approach to Insight in Psycho-Analysis and Groups* (1970). (See, for example, the section called *Reality Sensuous and Psychic)*. Partly because the 1967 account was so brief, but also for other more complicated factors, the deep connection to Freud's thought on the subject of dreams, on psychoanalytic method, and on the nature of the ego-functions underlying memory and attention, was not evident to many of those whose first reaction to Bion's presentation was one of rejection. Bion's ideas on the occluding effects of reliance in the analytic situation of memory and desires remain controversial in some quarters today, so it is enormously valuable that the original recording has been found of Bion's first presentation of these ideas, which were so important to him in his work and in his conception of a psychoanalytic attitude. I am indebted to the Archivist of the British Psychoanalytical Society, Joanne Halford for making the recording available to me to transcribe, and to Mr Kannan Navaratnem, the Editor of the *Bulletin of the British Psychoanalytical Society* in which the paper has first been published to be read by the membership of the Society to which the paper was first presented. I have written a longer Editor's Introduction to this paper because of its important place in Bion's thinking and because of the many serious misunderstandings to which the *Notes on Memory and Desire* has given rise.

I think it is of particular interest that in the full *Memory and Desire* talk, Bion mentions the analogy of 'artificial blinding' to which Freud referred in his letter to Lou Andreas-Salomé on May 25th, 1916. Although in the letter Freud referred to the act of writing, when he wrote, "I have to blind myself artificially in order to focus all the light on one dark spot, renouncing cohesion, harmony, rhetoric and everything which you call symbolic", it is clear that he was referring to psychoanalytic attention itself – the conditions necessary for the evenly-suspended attention which permits the analyst to 'turn his own unconscious like a receptive organ towards the transmitting unconscious of the patient'. (Freud, 1912 p. 115). In his May 25th 1916 letter Freud next refers directly to night vision:

> for my eyes, adapted as they are to the dark, probably can't stand strong light or an extensive range of vision.

The importance of this reference is significant for Bion's discussion of Memory and Desire in relation to Freud's own conjectures regarding the role of consciousness as a sense organ for the apprehension of psychical qualities. Freud (1900) had suggested, essentially, that there were two 'sensory surfaces' or envelopes feeding awareness, one receiving impressions of external reality through the senses and the other sensitive to impressions emanating endogenously. As well as stimuli from the perceptual system, consciousness can, suggested Freud, (see Solms, 1997).

> can receive excitations of pleasure and unpleasure, which prove to be almost the only psychical quality attaching to transpositions of energy in the inside of the apparatus. [Freud 1900, p. 574].

Bion meant his recommendations to dispossess oneself of past knowledge of the patient, as well as expectations and desire for his betterment, to be understood not only in relation to those of Freud (1912), but also with the principle described by John Keats as 'Negative Capability', and the corresponding 'apophatic'[2] approach of the early contemplative thinkers. These included the Dominican theologian and philosopher Eckhart von Hochheim, known as Meister Eckhart (1260–1328), and the Spanish Carmelite Friar, Juan de Yepes y Álvarez (1542–1591), better known as St John of the Cross.

The following extract, taken from a transcription of the recording of the discussion of Bion's *Catastrophic Change* paper at the Scientific Meeting on May 4th 1966, is included here because it illustrates so well an important aspect of Bion's recommendations on memory, desire and apperceptive understanding, when he referred to the ideas in his discussion on the pattern he called Container-Contained:

> **Dr Meltzer**:
> Now, when I listen to Dr Bion, I get drunk with a kind of delight because everything he says is so new, and so exciting, and I want to really express my resentment at this sort of drunkenness that he induces in me, and complain about how he does it, and why I think he shouldn't; and I want to agree with Dr Winnicott too, in that the chink is just where masterful chink detectors find it – it is when Dr Bion does not really condescend to inform us how it is linked with the things we have ordinarily been thinking, that he promotes in us a kind of excitement that takes us off, into new channels without providing us with an *anchorage*, and seems to me it affects us as if he were announcing messianic ideas. Now, it seems to me that it is necessary to grasp what he's talking about in terms of the history of psychoanalysis; and particularly I was struck by the anomaly of his wondering how it linked with the paranoid-schizoid and depressive positions, because it seems to me that it has a very clear link. In the history of Melanie Klein's work, for instance, it starts with the investigation of the genetic problems, the early phase of the Oedipus complex, it then went on to this

tremendous advance – I think the first advance in the economic aspect of metapsychology – the paranoid-schizoid and depressive positions, and this took her back into dynamic problems, connected with the discovery of projective identification, and that led her into a new investigation of instinct and the elaboration of the problem of envy, and this is the way it goes – it goes metapsychologically, from one area of metapsychology to another, and Dr Bion is now taking us back to the problem of structure.

Now as soon as I can recognise it, that he is taking us the next logical step from the advances posed by envy and gratitude, I stop being drunk and begin being really puzzled and worried about the quality of my work, and wonder what's wrong with it, that needs to be improved by what Dr Bion is talking about. Now of course I don't know, but it has something to do with structure of the mental apparatus. It seems to me that Dr Bion is talking about the kind of things that I have found myself, in times of worrying about, such as, where are the objects? Does the ego contain the objects, or does an object contain the ego? Or does the self contain them all? Really, what is the structure of the mental apparatus, and what is the significance of the continual getting in and out of one another that goes on within the different elements of the structure of the mental apparatus?

Following several other points of discussion:

Dr Bion:
To take up the point that Dr Meltzer made just now: I agree about this, and this is why when I spoke about the need to avoid the use of either Memory or to allow desire, as it were, also to develop, it was because I felt that it got between oneself and the patient; that there is something peculiar about the operations of what are normally understood as memory and desire which leave one particularly unfitted to intuit what is actually happening in the session, and I think it is related to this question of the anchorage, in that if you try to do this then I think you will have unpleasant and anxious experience, in which you feel you lose your anchorage; and one is constantly trying to find it; one is constantly trying to fall back on something or other like a cure or something of that sort, something with which one is familiar, as a protection against what is really an unpleasant situation, a situation in which anything may happen. The patient that you see tomorrow is a patient you've never seen before; why – because if you have seen them before, the problem has been dealt with. If he hasn't understood what you

> have said to him – if you haven't been able to introduce him to himself – it will turn up again, and what one wants to do is to deal with it in the form in which it turns up again, and not in the form in which one thought it turned up at some predetermined occasion which one has probably forgotten or imperfectly remembered anyway. Therefore it is important to see the patient tomorrow as if the patient has never been seen; it is a very difficult thing. It is much easier to talk about than to do; and the difficulty is made worse by this fact that one loses one's anchorage, and it's a nasty feeling, as you'll soon find out if you try that and if you have any success in trying it. Now, with regard to this feeling of excitement, well the point is that this subject is actually an exciting subject. And I think it is something that we all object to….

Essentially this part of the discussion relates to two forms of the relationship between the pattern of existing knowledge and the impact of new perceptions or ideas. Dr Meltzer, with his comment on mental 'anchorage' emphasises the desire for *apperception*, which, according to Johann Friedrich Herbart (1776–1841), is the process through which a collection of presentations becomes structured by the accretion of new elements, from the direction of sensuous reality or from thoughts. In this process there is an important quantum of reassurance stemming from the sum of antecedent experience, which compensates for the unsettling experience of new, unassimilated experience.

Apperception is thus a term for all mental processes in which a presentation is brought into connection with an already existing and systematized mental structure, and can thereby be classified, explained, understood. A later formulation by William James (1842–1910), based upon that of Herbart, is: "To unite and assimilate a new perception to a mass of ideas already possessed, and thereby to comprehend and interpret it."

Bion's formulations, on the other hand, stimulate the requirement of the reader or listener for *Negative Capability*, in which the links to an existing body of existing knowledge – represented in the paper as possessed and protected by a conservative containing group, or part of the mind, (called 'Establishment') – are set aside. Bion (1970, p. 125) quotes Keats's use of the term as it features in a letter the poet wrote to his brothers:[3]

> … several things dove-tailed in my mind, and at once it struck me what quality went to form a Man of Achievement, especially in Literature, and which Shakespeare possessed so enormously – I mean Negative Capability, that is, when a man is capable of being

> in uncertainties, mysteries, doubts, without any irritable reaching after fact and reason. [Quoted in Bion 1970, p. 125]

In his recommendations on *Memory and Desire*, Bion is suggesting the analyst tolerates the feelings consequent upon letting go, temporarily, of those facts and reasons forming the reassuring structure of existing theories and accepted facts, for the purpose of being receptive to new organisations of experience – what he has termed, borrowing from Poincaré, a 'selected fact' – essentially a fact that seems to select itself.

Parthenope Bion Talamo[4] (1981) put it in the following terms:

> This Selected Fact is one which the thinking individual recognizes as unexpectedly harmonizing all the other scattered facts – it is one of them, but it allows the thinker to "see" the meaning which had previously not been visible.

And in his 1967 *Commentary* to the papers of *Second Thoughts*, Bion wrote:

> The analyst must discern the underlying pattern by a process of discrimination and selection. If the account given is a selection made to demonstrate the correctness of the original selection, it is clearly worthless. Only if the original experience is a genuine evolution of a psychoanalytic realization, i.e. a precipitation of coherence by a "selected fact", does the writer's conscious discrimination and selection become legitimate as a method of representation.

In his contribution to the discussion (above) Donald Meltzer emphasised the not-uncommon subjective experience associated with the challenging demands made by communications in which explanatory 'anchoring' links, which allow *apperception* of the underlying pattern, are absent[5]. By referring to a sense of 'drunkenness' he is conveying the 'heady' effects of combined excitement and irritation which, according to Bion, have to be tolerated in analysis and in clinical thinking of a particular kind, and that the usefulness of doing so can be explored by the practising analyst if they wish to.

Bion underlined in his copy of *The Writings of St John of the Cross* Juan de Yepes y Álvarez the following sentences, and he labelled them in the margin as being relevant to his ideas on Memory and Desire. In order to appreciate the particular use to which Bion was applying these principles it is important to note that where there are references in such writings to God, or the 'Godhead', Bion is abstracting the term for use in his formulations in the realm of psychoanalysis, using analogical relations to bring out what he feels are detectable underlying patterns.

> All these sensory means and exercises of the faculties must be left behind and in silence [...] As a result one has to follow this method of disencumbering, emptying, and depriving the faculties of their natural rights and operations to make room for the inflow and illumination [...] If a person does not turn his eyes from his natural capacity, he will not attain to so lofty a communication; rather he will hinder it. If it is true that the soul must journey by knowing God through what He is not, rather than through what He is, it must journey, insofar as possible, by way of the denial and rejection of natural and supernatural apprehensions. This is our task now with the memory. We must draw it away from its natural props and capacities and raise it above itself (above all distinct knowledge and apprehensible possession) to supreme hope in the incomprehensible..... The annihilation of the memory in regard to all forms (including the five senses) is an absolute requirement [...] This union cannot be wrought without a complete separation of the memory from all forms [...] Once he has the habit ... he no longer experiences these lapses of memory in matters concerning his moral and natural life.
>
> (*The Writings of St John of the Cross*, Book 3, Ch 2, #2)

Where the mystical thinkers were attempting to find terms for the objects of *their* contemplation, which they did – in the examples selected by Bion for his purposes – by considering what their object of contemplation was *not*, Bion is attempting to use an analogous process for contemplating the non-sensuous psychic reality of psychoanalysis.

As Caper (1998) has pointed out, although Bion's expositions of Memory and Desire and his concept of O have been misunderstood by some analysts as signs of Bion having turned to mysticism, the formulations which Bion takes from mystical thinkers and applies to his formulations of container-contained (♀♂), the domain of O, and Memory and Desire constitute "a psychoanalytic model of mysticism, not a mystical model of psychoanalysis" [ibid., p. 420].

Finally, it is valuable to have available here the original 1965 paper *Memory and Desire*, in order to appreciate properly the linkages left out in the writing of his peremptory 1967 *Notes on Memory and Desire*, as well as offering further material that illuminates his discussions of psychoanalytic technique elsewhere in his work. It serves a similar bridging function in relation to his discussions in *Attention and Interpretation: A Scientific Approach to Insight in Psycho-Analysis and*

Groups (1970) and *Notes on Memory and Desire* (1967) as does his *Cogitations* in relation to the papers of the 1960s.

Notes

1 The discussants' comments have since been included in *Wilfred Bion: Los Angeles Seminars and Supervision* (2013), edited by Joseph Aguayo and Barnet D. Malin.
2 Enquiry proceeding by way of negation, considering what is *not*. As contrasted with 'cataphatic', proceeding by way of defining through positive statements, accumulative knowledge of what *is*; factual knowledge.
3 Keats J. (1817). Letter to George and Thomas Keats, 21st December 1817, *Letters of John Keats*, Harvard UP, Boston (1958).
4 *Rivista di Psicoanalisi*, 27: 626–628.
5 André Green, in his review of Bion's *Cogitations* (1992), made a roughly similar point, and welcomed these notes because they supplied some of the missing links to some of Bion's writings.

Paper II

Negative Capability[1]

W. R. Bion 1967

First I must apologize not to have been able to let you have a copy of this paper, which I really wanted to do, but it took much longer than I anticipated, so I hope that you can make something of what I want to convey to you this evening.

One point that I would like to make clear is that although it may seem strange – and I understand that what I write does seem strange – that really I don't think that I am saying anything that isn't already known. Therefore it would be helpful if people who get some sort of idea of what this paper is about, would try to match it with their own experience, because that is the important thing; not to be misled by any apparent strangeness in what I say, but to seek in it an expression of what you yourselves already say in your own way.

People often feel that I don't really give clinical examples. Now, I want to give as my clinical example, the session that you are going to have tomorrow with your patient. That is to say, a session that has not taken place. Which means that we all start fair. I say this as a point on which to focus attention, as it were; to consider it simply as a kind of prelude, to that session. One of the reasons that I want to do this is because I think that a difficulty which we do not always recognise is created for us, which is that we have to use a very inadequate form of communication with each other. I do not think that it is inadequate when it comes to the patient, because when one is giving an interpretation, the patient has a chance to know what we are talking *about*, and therefore there is always a chance that the patient will be able to use what we say in ordinary conversational English, which is what you use as you go along, because he has a chance of comparing it with what is actually taking place. When it comes to *lateral* communication, like we have here, it is a different matter, because I have to use ordinary English, or such improvement on it as I can manage, to talk about experiences which you haven't had, because they are experiences which existed between me and my patient, and, as everybody knows, you get a peculiar effect as a result of this. You get a situation in which you have no doubt, say, about an interpretation that you have given, and that was apposite at the time, and it is extraordinary to find that what you say [to colleagues] really causes no echoes, because what one says in the lateral communication is so *different*, and is so inadequate to describe what took place in the consulting room.

I think that one of the difficulties is that we are speaking through the medium of a language which is really related to experiences which are *sensible*, let's say which you can experience by virtue of your senses. But what we are *dealing with* is another matter. For example, we deal with anxiety. Nobody has the slightest doubt about the reality of anxiety, its existence; it is a fact. But, it cannot be seen or touched or anything of that sort, and yet we have to use the language which is really derived from things that we can touch and see. Now this is all very well when it is something like anxiety – you can talk about that amongst laymen, and they know what you mean, they have experience of it, and there is no difficulty. This also applies to ourselves, although over a very wide area because we happen to be trained analysts. But there are certain points, and I think that they arrive very quickly, where we float off the edge, as it were, of our vocabulary; that we are trying to talk of experiences, which we may all know, but which we experience differently. This is a serious matter because we very often have arguments and controversies in this Society, as we certainly ought to have, and they are growing points of any scientific development, but they are a waste of time because their apparent controversy is really stirred up through inadequate means of publication; that is to say, inadequate means for this lateral communication that I am talking about – communicating what one analyst has experienced, to somebody else who obviously has not had that experience, even if he thinks it is a similar experience. After all, by that time, you are quite a long way from the consulting room experience, which is very real, as everyone knows, and is quite unmistakeable. Now, I think that this really raises a question, which is quite impossible to talk about tonight. We cannot embark on the invention of a new language – that is a problem for the future. But there is no harm in remaining aware of the point and making allowances for the fact that we have this defective medium, and of possibly making some sort of approach, or trying to, or making a start at it, of finding a method of recording and communication which really does record and communicate.

This evening, we have the set-up for what you could call a scientific paper. This kind of thing [lateral communication] runs through everything that we do. It may be because psychoanalysis is such an extraordinary experience, and so unknown, that we like to cling to anything that we do know. And some of the things that we know about are seminars, supervisions, lectures and so forth, and we fall into the groove of using psychoanalytic modes of communication because it is quite bad enough – it is quite frightening enough – to do psychoanalysis without also embarking upon an educational system which is really felt to be strange and unknown. But the point that I would like to make, although the conditions do not exist for it, is that one should consider meetings of this kind – extra-sessional meetings – as being much more in the nature of 'games'. And, in doing this, to exploit what we know of children's games. I think that we should make use of our own discoveries in this respect, and the more we conceive of art which is played by children's games, the more we should exploit that knowledge in considering the evolution of our own educational systems.

Treating it in this way, I want to embark on a series of games of this kind, and I shall do it by trying first of all to give you a verbal transformation – as I like to call it – of a visual image. For example, the patient does what I am doing now, just scratches the wrist. It is a visual image, and I shall try to give you a verbal transformation of it. Now, let's try another one. This time there is somebody who complains about their wristwatch, and shows that there is an oedema – that the irritation is of such a kind that there is an oedematous swelling. Same story again. This time the patient has scratched their wrist to such an extent that there are scars, and these are signs that such scratching is very considerable. Now, the last version of this is of a patient who has threatened to slash their wrists, and is discovered, having actually done it, lying in a bath filled with blood, and is rushed into hospital. Now, let's go a bit further. Taking these visual images, let's formulate a 'theory',[2] or theme, and I would suggest that with the patient found lying in the bath, that their wound should be dressed, that they should be taken out, they should be prevented from doing it again, and in due course you should call it a day and discharge them. Now that is quite a satisfactory 'theory' for certain types of treatment and for certain people, for example the nursing staff or the psychiatric hospital. When it comes to psychoanalysis though, this won't do. It won't do because none of us really believes that such a patient is 'cured' or that the problem has been dealt with. It is an adequate 'theory' as far as it goes, but it is not adequate from our point of view.

I'd like to go on from there, taking the same sort of form, although it is awkward to do it in these conditions, but it is still a part of a game, introducing what I call a 'beast sense' – meaning by that what is usually meant by mathematicians. And I will suggest then that one regards the visual image that I have been putting to you, the total one, of any of these, as having a *direction*. You can either regard it that the patient has slashed their wrist from there [illustrates with gesture], or that it is from the inside *outwards*. I think that this begins to have a bit more meaning from the point of view of an analyst. The previous theory, which led simply to the binding up of the wrists and the saving of the patient from further damage, won't do for us, but I think that this sort of idea does. So I would like to suggest that one thinks in terms of direction: direction, as it were, of the visual image, in any or all of the four versions that I have mentioned, as being whole events which might be regarded as having a direction. I have also said, already, *inside* and *outside*, which is introducing another theory – that there *is* an inside and an outside. These things are applicable. They are derived from Space as we know it, but what relationship they have to the mind I do not know. Has the mind got an inside or an outside? Has it got a boundary, and where is it?

Now these points are not really important in the ordinary way. But when you start dealing with disturbed patients, those approaching what we ordinarily call 'borderline' cases, then these points become important. One would like to know if there are any borders or limitations of the mind, or whatever it is that we think we are dealing with. This sort of game that I am proposing can be played over in a number of ways. For example, one could consider placing those visual images, or my verbal transformation of them, in particular orders, for example the order shall we say of its violence. Here again it is difficult, because you could take the order that I have actually given – the trifling scratching of the wrist at one extreme, and the suicidal attempt at the other, putting them in that order. The first two cases and the theories that I have proposed about them, are not really particularly applicable to our work, but when it comes to the others they are much nearer the kind of thing that we have to deal with. But, once more, if you take what I have been saying this evening, the order of violence could also be dictated by the violence of the *communication*. For example, just to do that [Bion indicates scratching] is not likely to excite anybody's interest very much. But if you take the last instance, I think that anybody hearing me giving this account would *feel* that they are being presented with a verbal transformation which is *itself* violent. If you take the *scene* itself, presented by that patient to the nursing staff, that is also violent. That is a violent assault on the sense-apparatus of the staff. So, in considering this point about violence, we might consider there how much it is a matter of a violent assault, and if so, why. Has the patient got to make a violent communication of that kind because it is the only way of penetrating into the minds, and so forth, of those people amongst whom she lived and moved and had her being? In all this I am not suggesting any answers. I am merely suggesting a method of playing a game producing questions. One can continue with this theme of violence and ask oneself again whether it is violence of action.

I said that this was about tomorrow's session. But we haven't got the slightest idea what will happen in tomorrow's session. We therefore do not know anything at all about it. As psychoanalysts we are so used to 'seeing' things that are not ordinarily seen, that we forget how problematic this is. How great a problem it is to be able to 'see' whatever it will be that we will be able to see tomorrow. I don't want to take this idea of a game further now, but I do want to suggest that such a game is a sophisticated version of the child's game, which – as I say – we can exploit for purposes of exercising our minds for doing whatever it is that a child *does*. I suggest that it is related to the process of the psychoanalyst's growth. What about this session tomorrow? Here I want to read you a scrap, out of Freud's correspondence. It is a letter to Lou Andreas-Salomé, of May 25th 1916.[3]

> I know that in writing I have to blind myself artificially in order to focus all the light on one dark spot, renouncing cohesion, harmony, edifying effects, and everything which you call symbolic, frightened as I am by the experience that any such claim or expectation carries within it the danger of distorting the truth even though it may embellish it.

Here again, of course one risks misinterpreting what Freud wrote, that's a misfortune of this subject, but I must say that to me it has meaning that is valuable. I think that when it comes to the actual session, what we suffer from is not so much the lack of knowledge, lack of theories, lack of training, as too much knowledge, too much theory, and too much light. For this particular search in which we are engaged, I do not think of a *bright* light, if I can use this model, as to get the situation so *obscure* that the dimmest object, the faintest scrap of light, will show up. Therefore the important thing is to be able to exclude as much as you can, in order to bring a penetrating shaft of darkness to bear on the obscure spot.[4] I am not claiming for this any kind of universal validity, because I think that this sort of point will have to be settled by individual analysts. If you think that there is anything in this, then you can try it, and decide whether it has got anything in it or not. But the reason I am passing it on is that it seems to me to be valuable.

I would like to read another quotation, and this is from a letter by Keats to his brothers, which he wrote in December 21st 1817.

> several things dove-tailed in my mind, and at once it struck me what quality went to form a Man of Achievement, especially in Literature, and which Shakespeare possessed so enormously – I mean Negative Capability, that is, when a man is capable of being in uncertainties, mysteries, doubts, without any irritable reaching after fact and reason. Coleridge, for instance, would let go by a fine isolated verisimilitude caught from the Penetralium of mystery, from being incapable of remaining content with half-knowledge.

That is what I want to use this term, Negative Capability, for. I hasten to add that I do not want to add any more technical terms to psychoanalysis but it is a convenient way of summing up things, and leading you to understand that this is what I mean when I use the term – a capacity for tolerating half-truths as being essential to the Man of Achievement. Now, this point I also think is very important, because as analysts we are not free-wheeling. We do not want to have sessions in which there is plenty of conversation, free-association, interpretation and so on, but no achievement. And it gives a clue – only a clue – but something that we can follow up, to making a distinction between these everlasting (or nearly everlasting) analyses, of which I have had my share, in which nothing particular seems to happen, and which I certainly could not be satisfied with having deserved any of the results, from the co-operation between myself and the patient. But if one considers this point about Negative Capability, and if one regards the capacity to tolerate half-truth, uncertainties, mysteries, doubts, *without* any irritable reaching after fact and reason – this point is important, because when one gets into a situation like this, one finds sooner or later, usually sooner, that one finds it difficult to tolerate, and one starts reaching out for psychoanalytic interpretation. That, I think, is wrong. I think that it might be perfectly alright for a sort of conversational to and fro, but not for the analysis as *achievement*. If it is intended that the conversation should be a part of an exchange of achievement, then it is important that one should be able oneself to tolerate that, and important that the patient likewise should be able to tolerate half-truths and so on. Seeing them for half-truths, seeing them for mysteries and so forth, but being capable of tolerating them.

This leads to the point that I have discussed before, of the importance of Memory and Desire. What I want to suggest about this is a really very simple exercise. Instead of me telling you what I mean by Memory and Desire, I think that it would be a good thing just to try out doing without too much intrusion of whether or not it is nearly the end of the session. It is helpful if one can relegate that to mechanical means, a clock which one can see or something of that sort, so that it doesn't distract the patient, obviously. There are one or two points of this kind which are helpful, and which are easily dealt with, But if you allow these to obtrude, and for the habit to grow, for thinking about the end of the session, the end of the week, the weekend break and so forth, then one seems to introduce something which is *opaque*. It seems to have a capacity for getting between oneself and these queer things like anxiety, depression and so on, which we are trying to observe. This was brought home to me by a very disturbed patient who, I recognised, was constantly stimulating me to try to think what he has said, or I have said, on some previous occasion, and to stimulate me to want to 'cure' him or to do something or another for him, to do something other than psychoanalysis. And this is where one gets into difficulties, because it is so difficult to avoid the feeling that one really wants to *do* something for one's patient. Even in surgery this has been spotted, and it is not going to be a good thing for a surgeon to be over-concerned with the welfare of the patient as opposed to being concerned with the welfare of the operation.

I think that one should be in no hurry about this, but one should gradually in this kind of way come to one's own definition of what is meant by Memory and Desire. And then, when you feel tolerably certain that you have got a good idea about what is meant by this, using the two terms as interchangeable – Memory as being the past tense of Desire, and Desire as the future tense of Memory – then one can consider extending this to things that are not simply of a trivial nature. But the curve, as it were, rises very steeply. It is pretty easy to do it to the point that I am talking about, well enough to get clear about one's own definition – one's definition of Memory and Desire – it is not so easy to know where the process should stop. This point is a very important one. I don't think that everybody should try it. I would certainly hesitate to say that it is for anybody but psychoanalysts. And the reason for this is that it certainly does seem to make the experience a powerful one. At first sight one's anxieties about this, one's feeling that one ought to know what a patient has said, or what one has felt and so on, all seem to be very plausible, they have all got substance; otherwise they wouldn't be plausible, but the general effect, I think, is to intensify the analytic experience very much. So much indeed, that the psychoanalysis of patients moves into the centre of the analyst's life. And you get an effect which is rather similar to being analysed, in the same way that one's analyst is always a very important person, and this is reflected in dreams and such-like, in the same way the *practice* begins to be reflected in the analyst's dreams, and so on. And I think that it becomes possible to focus more on the origin of these various anxieties which appear all to have a sensible and understandable relation, by recognising the possibility that in fact they derive from the intense experience not of being psychoanalysed, but of psychoanalysing.

Something which would be more familiar to those who use Kleinian theories is, that if you are going to face your patient tomorrow, as near as possible (and you can't get nearer than that, but it is worth trying) then you get a situation in which what is going on in the analysis is the whole lot of discrete and meaningless episodes, in which the pattern is not discernible. Now that is difficult to tolerate, it requires Negative Capability. Otherwise one will rush in with an interpretation to get out of the dilemma of tolerating mysteries, half-truths, and so on. It is rather like looking through a kaleidoscope, with a whole mass of scraps and pieces. You give it a pat and you can see a pattern emerge. It is rather like that, as far as any model can describe it.

I'd like to make a distinction between this experience, which I call an *evolution*, and the experience which I call memory, which is one in which, as it were, one mentally scratches one's head and tries to think up something or another that has happened in the past – it is quite different. This is something which comes out of the situation; it evolves during the session. When that happens it becomes much easier to give a convincing interpretation because you are actually talking about something. It is also easier for the patient – although they may not realise it – because the analyst is talking about something which is available to the patient; if one's interpretation is correct then the patient *can* see it. It shows itself in this way where you feel there is a patient who, after denying what you are saying, comes the next day apparently having made quite a lot of progress. I think that it is because the analyst has been talking about something which was available to the patient, and therefore the penny did, ultimately, drop, even before the next session. But I think that it is useful to make a distinction there between what I have called evolution, and the thing that I have called memory.

To return to what I have been talking about, does this kaleidoscopic situation really correspond, also, to what Melanie Klein called a paranoid-schizoid position? And I feel that one must expect to have a peculiar experience in analysis, in which one moves from a sort of paranoid-schizoid position to a *depressive* position. For every interpretation you pass through both of these. The trouble is that these are terms of psychopathology, and as such one hopes that they are not really applicable. On the other hand I think that it would be a brave analyst who says that he is so well-orientated and so forth that he cannot have pathological mechanisms. So it is rather more in hope than in any expression of conviction that I would like to make a sort of *parallel* to movement from paranoid-schizoid to depressive, using terms like *patience* – for the paranoid-schizoid position, and *security* for the depressive position. That is to say, if one was an ideal analyst then one would pass through the phase of being patient (I use that term particularly because I want to retain the idea of trouble in it) to this other position of being secure, retaining also the meaning of it as being without anxiety, without care in that way I would suggest that the analysis becomes a dynamic experience for the analyst himself, and his *growth*. And, he is more likely, in my opinion, to recognise what is taking place and be able to get the patient to recognise it too, because one is not talking about an abstraction – whether one is using abstract terms or not. One is using defective language anyhow. The nearer it is to what is actually going on, the more likely it is to carry conviction.

I said that I would not advocate this for everybody. I think that one ought to proceed cautiously, setting one's sights pretty low – especially on this question of Memory and Desire, of suppressing them or getting rid of them – because, in a very extreme form, this comes awfully near to what the psychotic does. It is an attempt to defend himself against over-stimulation by the world of reality. It rather takes the form of destroying his ability to have any contact with stimuli from the real world, and it plunges him into a contact which is far too intense a stand with what we ordinarily call the Unconscious. So this procedure, as I say, ought to be used with caution; it ought to be used only by people who have had analysis, and, as I say, without being in too much of a hurry – and, also, expecting to find repercussions of one's own attitude and outlook of a disagreeable kind.

I did hear, when I spoke of this before, that many people thought that it was an easy procedure: all that you did was to forget your work and not bother about it. Well it isn't. It is not that. It's a tougher discipline than that and it's a nasty one – anyhow for quite a long time. Perhaps forever, as far as I know.

To sum up, then, what I am drawing attention to here, is the importance of this state that I have called Negative Capability – or not a state, but a characteristic. I think it may even be useful to bear this idea in mind when it comes to the question of selecting people for training and so forth, if one can find any way by which one can assess the capacity of the individual – the amount, as it were, of Negative

Capability – then it may help to lead one to somebody who can be a psychoanalyst. I need hardly say that I think that it is very important, because my experience of analysis is that it is a very tough assignment indeed. And I don't think that it is the kind of thing that people can easily take up. You can read any amount you like, and learn any amount you like, but in the last resort the person who is prepared to live with patients for hour after hour has to be tough. I hope I have made clear to some extent what I mean by that.

Notes

1 Paper given without notes at a Scientific Meeting at the British Psychoanalytical Society on Wednesday 4th October 1967 [Ed.]. Copyright © 2014 by The Estate of W. R. Bion. Printed by the kind permission of Paterson Marsh Ltd and Francesca Bion.
2 Here, as Ronald Britton has clarified, Bion is describing a 'model', a term which Bion himself uses later in the paper, rather than a theory [Ed.].
3 Bion's recitation of the letter from memory differed just very slightly in one or two places from the version published in the Freud *Standard Edition* [Ed.].
4 Bion reversed the polarity here, so to speak, and spoke of wanting to focus a *concentrated beam of darkness* onto an area too well lit. He considered that the intuitive capacity necessary for discerning psychical realities relied upon a non-sensuous channel, referred to by John Milton in *Paradise Lost*, in a verse quoted frequently by Bion, as 'inward eyes' [Ed.].

Editor's postscript

Bion began the presentation of his ideas to his colleagues in the British Psychoanalytical Society by apologising for not having pre-circulated his paper. In fact, as was his way, there was no paper. Bion was following his usual preference at this time of his life, giving a fairly spontaneous spoken version of ideas which he had hand-written as a series of notes, which he called 'cogitations'. As he spoke he held these in his mind much as a jazz musician will collate syncopated phrases as navigational 'waypoints', as it were, not necessarily traversed in the sequence in which they first arose in his mind when he had first noted them. Accordingly, he really did mean it when sometimes he began a talk by saying that he looked forward to discovering what it was that he was going to say.

He was curious to find out what his colleagues would make of what he was about to describe, which, basically, was his own way of doing psychoanalysis, his psychoanalytical attitude, to use a phrase of Melanie Klein's. Since 1965, when he had first communicated the gist of these ideas, expressed as the suppression or suspension of the analyst's own memory and desire, some analysts had misunderstood him radically, and this was particularly the case when he discussed with American colleagues his gnomic (unwisely so in my opinion) two-page *Notes on Memory and Desire.* Until the transcription and publication in 2014 of his fuller 1965 account, *Memory and Desire,* readers only had access to the didactic and rather 'gung-ho' account of Bion's methodological principle. In *Negative Capability* it is clear that he really did want his ideas to be received clearly, and the degree of preparation is evident. The paper should be read alongside the 1965 paper on *Memory and Desire,* to which it stands as a companion piece, as the two taken together offer a greater degree of depth, than the two-page *Notes* article.

As he had done two years earlier when presenting the 1965 paper, Bion oriented his listeners to reflecting upon the meeting they would have the following day with a patient with whom they might consider themselves *familiar*. He felt there to be something unique about the encounter that was very hard to convey to colleagues, not only because their way of doing analysis might differ, but because of the limitations of language to communicate certain real but ineffable dimensions of the experience itself. This he referred to, here and elsewhere, as the problem of lateral communication. The purpose of this reminder was to set the stage for a consideration of making the analysis with the patient real, by basing interpretations on experiences available to both analyst and patient in the immediacy of the events occurring in the session itself. This, we should note, is not identical to the transference and countertransference.

After exploring with his audience what he called a 'psychoanalytic game', really a 'thought experiment', involving scratching and cutting with differing degrees of violence, Bion introduced two thoughts of his own, based implicitly on the fact that all analysts, whatever their theoretical differences and preferences, made use of the deconstructive approach recommended by Freud called evenly suspended, or pending, attention (*gleichschwebende Aufmerksamkeit*).

Firstly, that in listening to a scene described by a patient in analysis we are not constrained to the order or direction of events put to us by the 'narrativised' organisation presented to us by the patient. The *directionality* of events was what Bion chose to consider in his talk. Secondly, although an account by the patient might depict actual, concrete violence, Bion suggested that the analyst might also bear in mind the communicative force or violence employed in and induced in the analyst *by* the description. Reading his paper the reader can appreciate the emphasis Bion is placing on evenly suspended attention even though he does not use the term, and, similarly, the implicit emphasis on the evocative and communicative uses of the mechanism of projective identification.

The scenes discussed by Bion he regarded as verbal and pictorial *transformations*, which had been his original contribution in his 1965 book of that title. He reminded the audience that a transformation including mental violence can be employed for what he sometimes called *hyperbole*, following his landmark findings put forward in his 1959 *Attacks on Linking*. This is how he put across that concept here:

> Has the patient got to make a violent communication of that kind because it is the only way of penetrating into the minds, and so forth, of those people amongst whom she lived and moved and had her being?

From here Bion moves in the paper to two quoted extracts from letters, one from Freud to his friend and colleague Lou Andreas-Salomé, and the other from the poet John Keats to his brothers, both which were of direct relevance to the main theme of his paper. He read first from Freud's letter:

> I know that in writing I have to blind myself artificially in order to focus all the light on one dark spot, renouncing cohesion, harmony, edifying effects, and everything which you call symbolic, frightened as I am by the experience that any such claim or expectation carries within it the danger of distorting the truth even though it may embellish it.

Relating this to negative capability, Bion suggested that there is very often insufficient ignorance in a session, rather than insufficient knowledge of the patient. He then read from a letter by Keats to his brothers, which he wrote in December 21st 1817:

> …several things dove-tailed in my mind, and at once it struck me what quality went to form a Man of Achievement, especially in Literature, and which Shakespeare possessed so enormously – I mean Negative Capability, that is, when a man is capable of being in uncertainties, mysteries, doubts, without any irritable reaching after fact and reason. Coleridge, for instance, would let go by a fine isolated verisimilitude caught from the Penetralium of mystery, from being incapable of remaining content with half-knowledge.

It had been the phrases, "being incapable of remaining content with half-knowledge" and "capable of being in uncertainties, mysteries, doubts, without any irritable reaching after fact and reason", which originally had caught Bion's eye when he was reading his book of the poet's letters. He had also been very taken with the term *Language of Achievement* as applied by Keats to the fundamental dramaturgical attitude of Shakespeare, because it corresponded well with Bion's appreciation, as an analyst, of the lack of an aim of moral judgement and moral education in the plays of Shakespeare, particularly the tragedies. Bion often made the point that what we seek in psychoanalysis is the language of achievement as distinct from the language of cause and the language of blame.

Readers will recognise in Bion's descriptions of his application to psychoanalysis of Keats's term a return to the basic method of radical openness, structural deconstruction and 'non-action' recommended by

Freud to enable contact with the Unconscious, and in the paper this is carried forward by Bion's explicit link between negative capability and the subjugation by the analyst of memory and desire. Perhaps to take into account some of the concerns of colleagues in the training organisation, he acknowledged the increased burden of difficulty and intensity resulting from suspending memory and desire, even accepting that it might not be found tolerable at the outset of learning to practice analysis. He did, however, retain his belief that real analysis necessitated the witholding of memory, desire and apperception. He gave sober warnings of its difficulty and intensity. Instead he suggested it as something for experienced analysts to explore. He said that the effect of suspending manifestations of memory and desire – particularly the desire to cure or to better the patient in some way, or to educate them, or even to keep firmly in mind what one previously has established as knowledge about the patient – was to:

> intensify the analytic experience very much. So much indeed, that the psychoanalysis of patients moves into the centre of the analyst's life. And you get an effect which is rather similar to being analysed, in the same way that one's analyst is always a very important person, and this is reflected in dreams and such-like, in the same way the practice begins to be reflected in the analyst's dreams, and so on. And I think that it becomes possible to focus more on the origin of these various anxieties which appear all to have a sensible and understandable relation, by recognising the possibility that in fact they derive from the intense experience not of being psychoanalysed, but of psychoanalysing.

As he had done on a previous occasion, when met with incomprehension over the issue of suspending the operation of memory, Bion made a distinction between conventional memory and a version of it which he called *evolution*. These are stored elements which seem to 'swim up' without the analyst seeking them out or calling them up. It is also similar to what Proust refers to, in his *Remembrance of Things Past*, as 'involuntary memory'. Bion's clarification of this issue was an attempt to make his ideas a little less counter-intuitive to his colleagues.

Bion used the analogy of a kaleidoscopic pattern to depict the initially disorganised array, or emotional pattern, presented to the receptive mind of the analyst employing negative capability and suspending the normal operation of the senses, understanding, and the accompanying memory and desire. The analogy allowed Bion to relate Melanie Klein's concepts of the paranoid-schizoid position and the depressive position. In Bion's hands these became extended into a principle of the organisation of perceptions, something that he had signalled in advance in his 1961 paper, *The Conception of Man*. There he had written, "The theory of projective identification and those derived from it explain more than what their propounder intended". Bion explained that the practice of negative capability for the analyst was an arduous one because it necessarily involved oscillating in the session between sharpened experiences which corresponded in some analogous way to the emotional positions described by Klein as stemming in all of us from the situations of early infancy.

In the paper Bion explains that the condition of negative capability means that before, during, and after each interpretation, the analyst passes through both of these dynamic situations, which in order not to conflate them with Klein's concepts, he gave the terms 'patience' (Ps) and 'security' (→ D) . In this way, said Bion,

> the analysis becomes a dynamic experience for the analyst himself, and his growth. And, he is more likely, in my opinion, to recognise what is taking place and be able to get the patient to recognise it too, because one is not talking about an abstraction – whether one is using abstract terms or not.

Bion ended his paper by reminding his colleagues that suspending memory was not an 'easy touch', allowing us to conceal laziness by representing it as a technical procedure.

"Well, it isn't", he said, pointedly. "It is not that. It's a tougher discipline than that and it's a nasty one – anyhow for quite a long time. Perhaps forever, as far as I know." Following the presentation of his ideas, and before coffee and discussion, Donald Winnicott, who as President of the Society was chairing the meeting, spoke movingly to Bion:

> We seem to be in the process of learning new techniques. Dr Bion will I hope remember when he goes abroad that he is still a member of this Society and that we count on him to come back, and give these papers of this kind, which is one of a series, and it is a tremendous loss to us to have Dr Bion going, and he's just got to remember that we shan't forget him.

Paper III

Break Up, Break Down, Break Through[1]

W. R. Bion 1975

As I was listening to the introduction to my talk I had the uneasy feeling of excitement and anticipation to the point that I could hardly wait to hear what I was going to say. As time passes, I have the dreadful realisation that I am supposed to be doing the talking as well. However, I would like to add a little bit more to the title: namely, Break In or Break Out. There is the big question of how much or how many of those things?

The first point I want to make, and to say it clearly, is: What is it like being confronted with an *unknown* situation? By 'unknown situation' I mean any situation in which we meet a person for the first time. I think of this as a situation in which one needs to denude oneself of memories and desires – taking memory as everything that is past-tense, such as history and so forth; all that one has learned; what one has been taught; and what one has picked up, the accumulation of experience over the course of one's life. Desire, then, is thinking of what is going to happen.

It seems to me that over and over again, both of those states of mind adorn a kind of screen between oneself and an experience, or a subject, which confronts us in its immediacy. If there are memories which produce a particular preconception, one already is waiting *for* something that one expects to hear, and that situation, therefore, is one in which one has to make a choice. But, in choosing, you also choose what you are *not* going to be aware of, so the memory, whatever it is, draws a screen in front of you – a screen of preconceptions which makes it difficult to observe anything which lies outside that area. The same thing is true for desire. The moment you start thinking what you would like, and what you hope for, thoughts about that get in the way, and once again you cannot be open to what is going on.

I hope that sounds fairly simple. In practice, however, it is not. This situation – of choosing what you are going to attend to – also involves *inhibition*. It is of course important to have some kind of preconception, but we must also be able to discard it, and also to be able to find some method of doubting the inhibition, particularly if it becomes rigid or fixed. Freud points out that most of these ideas and theories have, at some point, been conscious. Even a small child forms ideas, and it does not matter much if at one moment there is a temporary sense of certainty amongst the ideas – the person is able to change his ideas and obtain a kind of mental mobility. But the trouble can happen when we feel we possess a 'fact'. Once we have an idea that we actually can 'see' something, and that what we can 'see' is a fact, we *stick* to that idea. Then it becomes used as a kind of *preconception*, and it becomes an important matter for us to maintain it, as something fixed.

For example, as we now know, it is quite easy to take a biological view of the human being, in which we are beings very much affected by the sexual impulse, so much so that one borrows a term like that (impulse) from the anatomists and physiologists . There is very little to be said about sex as far as anatomy and physiology are concerned. All human beings have become acquainted with sex, at one time or another, from an early age. A difficulty arises for our thinking if there really is something that we can, legitimately, call a mind, a character, a personality. If, in the mind or the personality of the individual, there is sexual development analogous to the physical development, we do not really know what this is, whereas sexual maturity is a meaningful term when we are talking about anatomy and physiology. I do not think it is meaningful in talking about a type of personality. We do not know what this mind is.

Historically, it took a long time to link mind or personality with the brain, and a very long time after that to associate it with thinking. The theories are plausible: If you consider the idea of a mind or character portrayed in Homer or Virgil, you get an impression of particular kinds of belief that have gone into the thinking – the location of the mind or personality in the diaphragm, for example. If someone is showing emotion, very strong feelings, there is a tendency to breathe out. It is plausible to suppose that all of that is produced by this thing [touches his chest] which goes jogging up and down; you can assume that anatomical explanation of thinking, and that anatomical location of the centre of thought. As usual, somebody is sure to invent another idea, and the obvious temptation is to get rid of the rival idea.

Even the individual person hates housing or developing a new idea, because if you do, it is inevitable that you feel you *should* have got it right the last time. The inevitable discovery that you have been mistaken is a dreadful thing to discover. It also carries with it the feeling that if your own ideas change, then all the problems that you have ever solved are re-opened because they have a relationship of things-not-oneself with oneself[2]. You can appreciate how confusing this gets.

If the other is not a thing-in-itself, but another person just like one-self, then they are to some extent a thinking being. You then get this extraordinary theory of how these two people are to come together. Suppose they have different ideas or a different language, or a different method of expression. Suppose their methods of expression also throw some light on the way that they *think*. If, for example, you are dealing with people used to using articulate expressions and articulate thought, you naturally enough make the assumption that most people do so. But if we suppose that the individual is, say, Chinese, or someone who lived many hundreds of years ago, it is doubtful that we could conclude that they would think in the same way. Supposing someone sees things in 'Tao' and they invent a method of communication based on visual images. Is one to assume that the sort of thinking which is represented, say, by a Chinese person, derived from pictograms, symbols made of lines drawn around some kind of thought or idea – is one right to assume that they are put together in the same sort of way as we do with the symbols and phrases that we use in articulate or logical thinking? A great deal of misunderstanding arises simply by assuming that it is so, and attempting to translate these communications as though they were logical communications following the laws of logic, or the rules of grammar with which one is familiar in most western cultures.

For a time, Freud took up Rank's theories about the Birth Trauma. Rank developed his theories strictly in accordance with the principle that I have suggested: having had an idea, we hate to have to start on another one. It therefore feels much better to go on developing the scheme that we thought of; so you get a spicket[3] running. Freud turned his back on the idea of his Birth Trauma, but Rank went on developing it in a direction that does not seem to me to have been very fruitful. But what he said is that this impressive sojourn of birth would seem to split-off the ante-natal mode, of thinking or being – although he did not quite say it in this way – from the post-natal. It sometimes seems to me easier to understand what we are confronted by if we imagine that there is some kind of *carry-over of something*. I do not know what to call that something. Freud's ideas about the Unconscious do not seem to be of much help here, they do not seem to be applicable to the 'thoughts' and feelings of the foetus. It may seem even more ridiculous if one thinks of it in anatomical terms, thinking of the embryological optic pits or the auditory pits, realising that even the foetus may be subjected to pressures inside the womb, giving rise to something similar to what happens to you when you press on your eyeball with your finger. You get an impression of light, in a way that is distinct from the impression of light that comes from an external source of illumination. It is possible that the foetus at some stage becomes aware of what I am forced to call 'sight'.[4] Later on there would be what we could call 'sense impressions'. If at this point we fall back on anatomy and physiology, at what point would it be said that the sense of sight develops in the infant? All one says is that it does not, and that it is after birth that the baby sees things. This separation may be important to that particular 'diaphragm', namely the particular division between ante-natal and post-natal. It is a difficult question, but it does not matter much to us psychoanalysts, because we limit ourselves to talking, and attending to a conscious relationship with another conscious being. The division between Conscious and Unconscious is a valuable distinction, but here again, what may be very useful to us talkative human beings may have nothing to do with Reality, whatever that is. Science is very useful to us. What is scientific is that little bit which lies within the comprehension of the human being. In a dream-like way we assume that the universe is formed in the sort of way that obliges our capacities for thinking.[5]

Assuming that there really is a phenomenon, and not only a concept, called a mind, or a personality, or a character, and all the thoughts possible to that mind arose to make possible a literature on psychoanalysis. Is that correct? But then we have to consider again: who is it that I and he, or she, reads? Or when I and 'it' reads? Then there is the question of you and me. That means there is something assumed to be very like my own thoughts, and that the others who can think and feel are imagined as similar to what one thinks of *being oneself*. The whole elaboration of psychoanalytic theory depends on the axiom that one knows that there is such a thing as a mind. Why not assume that the foetus has a mind – or the child, or the adolescent?

Freud theorised on the distinction between the modes of operations of the conscious and the unconscious systems of the mind, but he seemed also to respect that people might be thinking unconsciously, even during sleep. He developed a series of theories from what the person reported having dreamt. It is worth remembering that by the time they have reported it, we do not in fact know the dream itself. "I dreamed last night…", and the patient conveys to us a verbalised series of pictorial images. To reiterate, they paint us a verbal *version* [6] of pictorial images. An artist could draw it for you. The dreamer seems to be able to put a line around this extraordinary experience that he has had in his sleep. He even puts a line around an experience that he had when he was awake.

An artist will draw a portrait of somebody. I have known occasions where important people have become extremely angry and have become destructive at their portrait,[7] but what they got angry about is another matter, and what an artist is thinking is another matter. To take another kind of artist, the musician, we sometimes encounter a person who says, "I do not know what you are talking about with your words, and I cannot make words to tell you what I think, but if you had a violin here, I could play it to you". There is a notation for the communications in that medium. The people who write these signs on paper make music with one another. Occasionally one comes across someone who cannot stand the piano. I have known a person who could not bear to hear what I know to be one of the best symphony orchestras in existence. I did not think that music could be hated, but there is no good reason for my supposition. The person was a cultured individual but he found it impossible to go to any performance because it caused him intolerable mental pain. I have come across something similar, a person who could not bear to draw or to paint, and someone who could only wear a particular outfit because there were colours which he could not stand to have close to his skin. I have come to feel that it is very important to be wide open to these sense impressions. If someone describes something that they see, you can vocalise your knowledge and it may or may not be right. And say the person is hallucinating, suppose they have access to remnants of mind which one would have thought had ceased to exist at birth, that existed before then? What if these are reminiscences of a still-existing part of the mind because the person still is aware of foetal impressions?

If you suspect something of that kind it can be discussed theoretically, but in the consulting room what are you going to say to them? First of all, what are you going to allow yourself to be aware of? It is easy to say, "Oh well, this patient is talking to me of his foetal level of mind". Would it be awful if it turns out that there is such a thing as non-sense, and that there are methods of linkage that are not rational? The mathematicians seem more tolerant of this when they talk of the rational numbers, for example, and even a kind of 'grammar', but I think that what they are doing is similar to the intuitionists, who step outside the boundaries of their subject.

Sometimes someone listens to a concert on the radio and is not concerned about the music because they are concentrating instead on the interference. You realise that he is disturbed by something specific underlying his interest in the interference, and you open up a realm beyond the capacity of visual imagery and the kind of communication related to what can be seen. If you pay attention to what people say about their experience of singing, it is clear that they have emotional experiences which are not comprehensible to us. We can deal with this difference by concluding that they simply are 'gifted individuals', "They are geniuses, forget it!". And we do! After all, who bothers to read the work of geniuses? Some of us have to submit to it, as I did in order to read Shakespeare, with a great deal of anguish. I was lucky, because I began to think that there was something in it. So there is something to be said for going on and reading Shakespeare even if you do not have to. By that time, unfortunately, I received a whole mass of ideas about who and what Shakespeare was, and I needed to break through those formations of knowledge, in order to find my way back.

Sometimes a patient comes to see you and they say, "I have had a terrible time, I have had a great time". You are supposed to pay attention to that, if you are a doctor or a psychiatrist or a psychoanalyst. One might suspect that they have had an experience which they would refer to as a *breakdown*. Or they might say, "Well, you know, I am getting old, and I am breaking up". Can one make anything of this sense of directionality, perhaps by way of some sort of Cartesian co-ordinate system? In understanding the "Bi-Logical" aspects,[8] about coming *in*, going *out* etc., and other such representations of "in" and "out", there may be other types of emotional experience to which a "co-ordinate system" could be applied. I certainly could not do it, it requires a lot more knowledge than I have, but somebody might find a way of using it.

What happens when the baby is born? Who starts it? Does the baby break out of the mother's womb? Does it subsequently break out of various forms of thought? Let us say that it is quite used to thinking whatever it thinks and to finding a new bright idea. I remember seeing a child walk into an exhibition and saying, "Oh Mummy, look at the beautiful picture!", pointing up at it, and the mother replied, "Yes dear, come on". She did not want to hear this sort of thing from a child. The child learns that it is very unwise to have ideas of that sort. A beautiful picture that is not even a picture: the things themselves actually are the subject. So there is something wrong with it, there are plenty of 'reasons' to say the child is talking 'nonsense' if it is speaking a different language to the adult.

And then the child learns to feel that what is thought *as* a child is just nonsense. On this basis, you can yourself look back on ideas that you used to have, and to disapprove of them, and to cease to have any respect for what *you* have known. You can cease to have respect for, and belief in, your own mind – when it behaves in a way which does not fall in with 'the rules', the rules which as an adult you have learned to respect.

In reaching the various stages of development – latency, adolescence etc. – there are crudely defined states of mind which we can be said to have 'got into' and then become 'stuck in', unable to get out. At what point does an extreme rigidity of thought change into the state of mind which can tend towards uncharted ideas? In the dream state one can differentiate between these. It can become possible in scientific thinking or religious thinking. Not all distinctions that can be made amongst ideas, however, have their counterparts in reality. It is not always possible to draw the boundaries, and sometimes all we can say is that it is helpful to tolerate what we do not know – to be able to bear to be ignorant. I am not sure this is always possible.

We can always hit on an explanation which is simple, and does not require too much thought and therefore does not interfere too much with what we want to do. This applies also to theory, including mine, and you can stick with one until it becomes a kind of shell that you cannot break through. The shell can be so vulnerable and feeble that you are always afraid that you are going to have a break-down, or break-out, or something because, after all, the shell is a part of us and I object to some sort of change or other that is appearing in myself which is allowed to break out or break through. We hope to find some doctrine which will help us to reinforce that state of a shell in such a way that we get such a hard shell that there is no likelihood of breaking down or breaking through. But of course that is at the expense of the urge to have any ideas. If you are going to allow yourself to have any ideas, it would be important to retain the potential to be freely expressive and to be receptive to all the thoughts, feelings, and ideas that come up. And it is sure too to be *expensive* if we are in contact, in such a state, with other people who are not going to encourage it.

Notes

1 Presented as a talk followed by discussion, with members of The Study Centre for Organizational Leadership and Authority (SCOLA) in Los Angeles on 9th December 1975. It was transcribed from a tape recording made on the occasion.

2 In his final paper, *Making the Best of a Bad Job* (1979), Bion was to return to this. He wrote, "When I say 'scientific' in this context, I mean the process of realization as contrasted with the process at the other 'pole' of the same concept, ideal-ization, the feeling that the world, the thing, the person, is not adequate unless we alter our perception of that person or thing by idealizing it. Real-ization is doing the same thing when we feel that the ideal picture which we present by our statement is inadequate. *So we must consider what is the method of communication of Self with Self.*" (emphasis added [Ed.]).

3 A tap.
4 Here Bion is considering that early structures 'anticipate' their later function.
5 Bion had in mind here Heisenberg's statement: "The existing scientific concepts cover always only a very limited part of reality, and the other part that has not yet been understood is infinite. We have to remember that what we observe is not nature herself, but nature exposed to our method of questioning."
6 At the beginning of his 1965 book *Transformations: Change from Learning to Growth*, Bion – in this context of pictorial representation, introduced the concept of *transformation*. He was drawing on the early work of Wittgenstein and Russell [Ed.]
7 Bion is referring to Sir Winston Churchill, whom Bion believed had been very intensely distressed at what was revealed of him by a portrait painted by Graham Sutherland. (Historically, there are conflicting views of these events.) [Ed.]
8 A reference to the work of Ignacio Matte-Blanco (1975), *The Unconscious as Infinite Sets: An Essay in Bi-Logic*. London: Duckworth. Revised edition: London: Karnac, 1998 [Ed.]

Editor's postscript

This paper was given as a talk without notes to members of The Study Centre for Organizational Leadership and Authority (SCOLA) in Los Angeles on 9th December 1975, and was followed by discussion. It was transcribed from a tape recording made on the occasion.

Bion sometimes referred to some of the ideas contained in it in supervisions, lecture/discussions, and seminars in the United States, Brazil and Argentina. From the way he spoke of it, many clearly believed it to be a completed paper, but Bion never wrote it. It remained as a transcribed audio recording and no preparatory notes have been found. He really does seem to have valued the central ideas of his talk, but he did not work his ideas into a publishable paper.

In preparing the texts for *The Complete Works of W. R. Bion*, I made the decision as Editor, together with Francesca Bion as Consultant Editor, not to include this paper. We felt that too much work remained to be done in getting it to a publishable standard, and that if this were to be attempted, the work would not completely have been his own. With the experience of having completed the project, which included several incomplete texts (but on the whole of a higher standard of writing) as well as transcribed lectures and talks, I felt in a position to look again at this paper in the light of that editing experience. Comparing the text with those recorded instances in which Bion mentioned the ideas behind the paper, a task made possible by having a digitised version of the entire Complete Works, also helped.

I also brought to the task of re-reading it a greater appreciation of a shift of emphasis in Bion's psychoanalytical attitude, which he described in his book *Transformations* (1965). Traditionally, psychoanalysis has emphasised the aim of insight – a form of knowing. In *Transformations* Bion theorised about how interpretive work could potentially effect a transition from knowing to Being. He wrote:

> When, as psychoanalysts, we are concerned with the reality of the personality, there is more at stake than an exhortation to "know thyself, accept thyself, be thyself", because implicit in psychoanalytic procedure is the idea that this exhortation cannot be put into practice without the psychoanalytic experience. The point at issue is how to pass from 'knowing' 'phenomena' to 'being' that which is 'real'... Is it possible through psychoanalytic interpretation to effect a transition from knowing the phenomena of the real self to being the real self?
>
> Bion, W. R. *Transformations*, 1965, p. 148; (2014): 5: 259

From an existential perspective he argued that the phenomena we meet in the consulting room are aspects of knowledge, reached by what he termed 'transformations in K', whereas the reality of the patient is 'become', so in order to further psychic *growth*, psychoanalytic interpretation must move beyond accretion of knowledge. Although Bion understood that many colleagues would not believe attention to the patient's being and becoming to be an important part of psychoanalysis, he wanted to explore the potential for interpretive work in this area; he wanted to close the gap between knowing *about* psychoanalysis and *being analysed*, and the corresponding rift between knowing about the self and being real.

It is this latter initiative of Bion's that, in my opinion, justifies the editing work to enable the posthumous publication of the paper, together with a postscript that clarifies the two major strands of the work – the components of knowing and being – and how they belong together.

In the talk it is evident that Bion made his listeners wait quite a while before entering the theme of *breaking*, subjecting it (as in its title) to the variation of *directionality*. This I regard as his existential theme, one with immediacy and power in relation to the main traumatic events of his own life. He also incorporated ideas concerning brain phylogeny to discuss fundamental questions about the *being* of the self or the mind.

I can imagine – though this is speculation – that Bion might have held back in making this talk into a paper partly because its subject matter had a close bearing on his own sources of existential anxiety, firstly as a seven year old separated by a continent from his parents, and his loved Aya, who remained in India, and later in the First World War as a young man fighting in Northern France. Whether this is the case or not, he retains a link throughout the paper to existential anxiety, and in all of his work to what is unknown. At moments, notwithstanding his many recommendations about suspending attention to the already known, he appears perhaps to find temporary respite in the tangible specifics of Freud, sex and the brain. Eventually he delves into the more abstract realms of ideas of the self or the personality. He asks the kinds of existential questions posed by Samuel Beckett, who, in *Texts for Nothing*, wrote: "… who would I be, if I could be, what would I say, if I had a voice, who says this, saying it's me?" Bion, who in the 1930s had been Beckett's psychotherapist, asks similarly, who am I if I no longer hold the same ideas by which I defined myself? When he uses terms such as "things-not-oneself", and "thing-in-itself", he is firmly in the realm of existential ideas about modes of Being.

Bion writes of the feeling that,

> if your own ideas change, then all the problems that you have ever solved are re-opened because they have a relationship of things-not-oneself with oneself. You can appreciate how confusing this gets … If the other is not a thing-in-itself, but another person just like oneself, then they are to some extent a thinking being. You then get this extraordinary theory of how these two people are to come together.

He seems at this point to be deeply in touch with what, in Sartrean terms, could be described as his own existential nothingness. He expresses his recognition, with accompanying angst, that the self he had constructed based upon experience is now no longer the same self when he experiences the world differently. Bion expresses the turbulent emotions of this realisation which strikes him forcibly, as does his understanding of the impact of the experience of interacting with another who is not a thing but a being.

Bion then describes the anxiety about being able to trust anything as a *given* – language, symbols, meaning are all open to deconstruction and to two individuals having completely different experiences of the same phenomena, making even his sensory experience unreliable. Following these passages Bion's focus then shifts to pre-natal experience and the absolute unknown, and once more he seems to reach for the concrete. The idea that sense impressions that belong to him go back to those he experienced in the womb – they seem to constitute a searching for an essence to quell his anxiety at being nothing – his fear of breakdown is real[1] because at this point he is in touch with a truth – that of his own existential nothingness. Perhaps in approaching these turbulent truths Bion found himself employing psychoanalysis itself as what he would have called a defensive 'column 2' statement,[2] when he says "it does not matter much to us psychoanalysts", at the point at which the matter is too unbearable to stay with. But, interestingly, he cannot help but return to uncertainty, and when he brings in literature he seems very in touch with the deconstructionists and post-structural thinking, which considers texts having no fixed, essential meaning. His use of the analogy of the shell returns us to that which is fragile and breakable in life, putting us in touch not only with our specific, tangible fears, but also with the anxiety of not having a self that is entirely reliable.

Close to the end of his talk, Bion discusses *the directionality* of breaking. The importance of directionality had been an important theme of his original spoken version of his *Negative Capability* paper, presented in the Autumn of 1967. His point was that whatever might appear to be the familiar narrative, the 'natural' chain of events, we need to take an unprejudiced, evenly-suspended, attitude, especially to the potential *direction* of events taking place in psychical reality.

In 1977, in Italy, he said to a seminar group,

> The emotional turbulence which is initiated is of some consequence because all sorts of elements, to which we don't usually pay much attention and of which we are not aware, get churned up and thrown onto the surface. They are often so noticeable that we give them a name – I tried to summarize it in a talk called "Break Up, Break Down, Break Through". I could almost say, "Choose Your Own Preposition". But we as analysts should use these words carefully; if we are going to talk about "break down" or "break up", at least let us be clear in our own minds by which coordinate system we are measuring the direction of the break

This was said in an almost jaunty way, but the reader should be aware of the enormous salience of these phrases for Bion in terms of his life's experiences. He was taken with the analogies suggested by associated terms such as breaking up, breaking down, breaking through, outbreak, breaking out, and breaking in. The different terms, as he would say, using the terminology of David Hume, marked different constant conjunctions, many of which held psychoanalytic or psychiatric associations. His interest in catastrophic change and catastrophic anxiety also seems to have played a part in his orientation to his topic, as well as his feeling about the salience of directionality in the terms 'in' and 'out', 'into' and 'out-of', having been influenced by his Kleinian approach to introjection and projective identification, and the researches made possible by his well-known expansion of the latter in terms of a psychical *container* for anxiety and object relations.

Interestingly, Bion's first mention of the concept of *breaking through* is in relation to himself. It is a significant one, in terms of his later thinking, and appears in a touching passage in his autobiographical writings[3].

> Mrs Hamilton and Mrs Rhodes, both in their different ways, helped to make my last year at the prep school one in which *I began to break through what I see in retrospect to have been an intolerable exoskeleton of misery.* I did not see my parents; Hirst was inaccessible in his own misery which could not be eased by us; Miss Whybrow entertained hopes of an outlet for her ambitions through Hirst's calamitous situation and favouritized attractive boys like Freddie Sexton. I must have felt Mrs Hamilton's personality as Spring to my prep school Winter. [emphasis added]

Mrs Hamilton was the mother of one of Bion's two friends at that time. Bion's own mother was in India and he hardly saw her. Mrs Hamilton evidently was a warmly maternal woman and it is clear that the young Bion had rather fallen for her. He noted that, "on being shown her son's achievement, [she] burst into peals of the most fascinating and lovely laughter". Bion expresses himself clearly here. He knows that he has required help, from a maternal person, in order to be able to break through what he calls an 'exo-skeleton of misery', which he relates in part to his sustained separation from his parents. In the account Bion notes those external figures who, for various reasons of their own, were not able to be helpful containers for him, but Mrs Hamilton was emotionally available and he was able to make use of the good relationship. This help offers him a revitalising Spring from the emotional Winter of his depression. The surrounding context to his account makes clear that his inner state had undergone a revival not only in terms of a maternal presence, he also had felt reunited with a good internal version of the couple. Bion was to make use of the concept of an exo-skeleton later in his work.

Breaking out and breaking through were terms burned right into Bion from his war experiences as a young man fighting in the First World War. He makes many references to soldiers breaking through enemy lines, and the breaking out of violent hostilities. In The Long Weekend, for example:

> we have been told the enemy has to *break through* at no matter what cost. There's only you lot and this bunch of infantry between him and the sea thirty or forty miles behind. There are no orders

> for retreat because there is no retreat arranged. You hold on – unless of course you are dead …
>
> The entire trench system began to *break loose and start skywards* in great and little clods of earth. I was sure in my ignorance that the enemy had started a night attack – and in my ignorance I was quite correct.

And finally, in relation to warfare, from Bion's *War Memoirs*, there is this:

> 'He's in extremely good form', said Carter. 'He's quite convinced that this is IT, that we're going to break right through and end the war.'
>
> 'Ah, yes', said Hauser bitterly, 'this war, like the last war, is to be the war to end war; and the next war, like this war, will be a war to end war, and so on *ad infinitum*. And all the breakthroughs are the last possible breakthroughs which break through everything of course, naturally.'

In his 1943 paper *The War of Nerves*, Bion wrote of the break-up of morale in the civilian population assailed by anxiety about their survival.

> Again, the formation of coteries amongst the well-to-do would reflect itself rapidly in *a break-up of morale in the mass of civilians* who in some sense look to them for leadership. This would be particularly marked if the authorities in any A.R.P. district were felt to be split up into cliques. Morale may deteriorate if authorities are felt to be out of touch with subordinates.
>
> Bion, W. R. (2014); Vol. IV, p. 20

In the 1950s and early 1960s Bion worked with patients in psychotic states. He realised that many references made by his patients to a feared anticipated mental breakdown suggested that the underlying situation was of a breakdown that had already occurred. He also observed in several individuals that the course of their breakdowns were sometimes communicated as a highly condensed series of associations appearing within the same session. Of the example that he gave of such a condensed communication of a breakdown, Bion wrote:

> I have chosen this example because it gives a good idea of the way a patient will compress into a few associations the whole of a

> "break-down" which it has taken years to accomplish in the first instance; the experience against which he has mobilized so much of his resistance is now lived through with comparative ease. It shows how the depressive position can be used as an escape from the paranoid-schizoid position and vice versa; and it shows the part that is played in these changes by the integration and disintegration of verbal thought.

Before moving to Bion's two specific published references to his notes – on breaking up, down, through etc. (he made numerous mentions of the paper in supervisions) – I will mention one final, and very significant reference of his, to breaking down. This appears in his paper *A Theory of Thinking* (1967, p. 116), where he describes the severe mental consequences to the infant or small child of a breakdown in the mother's capacity to take in their anxieties and to contain them emotionally. In other words, a breakdown in her capacity for what he termed *reverie* :

> The tasks that the breakdown in the mother's capacity for reverie have left unfinished are imposed on the rudimentary consciousness; they are all in different degrees related to the function of correlation. The rudimentary consciousness cannot carry the burden placed on it. The establishment internally of a projective-identification-rejecting object means that instead of an understanding object the infant has a wilfully misunderstanding object – with which it is identified. Further, its psychic qualities are perceived by a precocious and fragile consciousness.

This passage is of the greatest importance for understanding many intractable and apparently recalcitrant situations in the everyday practice of psychoanalysis and psychotherapy. For those readers wanting to go further with this, there is a relevant discussion in his 1959 paper *Attacks on Linking*, under the section with the subtitle, *Denial of Normal Degrees of Projective Identification*. The breakdown in the mother's capacity or willingness for entering into the container-contained (♀♂) relation with her child precipitates and constitutes a mental catastrophe of unimaginable proportions, with a *break-up* of mental structure and the capacity to make links and symbols, a *breakdown* of the capacity to think and communicate, and a *breaking-through* into the damaged ego of newly formed damaging objects that ensue from the sense of an object refusing to convert the infant's projected self-in-distress into something bearable.

In his allusive psychoanalytic novel, *Memoir of the Future*, the characters assembled by Bion have the following conversation:

> **p.a.** (psychoanalyst): Any culture, civilization or temporarily exposed characteristic of persons or peoples is subject to penetration and displacement by the unexpected. They say animals are aware of the imminence of an earthquake. Humans are sensitive to the imminence of an emotional upheaval.
>
> **Alice**: You mean people who are afraid they are going mad, or going to have a breakdown?
>
> **Roland**: *Break up, down, in, out, or through?*
>
> **p.a.**: Yes, though I was thinking of being subject, as human animals, to a cosmic upheaval…

Referring to this passage, Martha Harris made the following reference to the "break-up, break down, break-through" of catastrophic anxiety, which is what Bion is indicating with the terms emotional turbulence, turmoil, and cosmic upheaval.

> Those of us with some experience of child analysis, and even of child rearing may be aware [of] how too intense an encounter with their hidden selves may be avoided by paramnesias, as he describes in his paper *On Evidence* (Bion, 1976). There are patients who may be successful in avoiding the unpleasant experience of "break-up, break down, break-through" of catastrophic change (Bion, 1991, p. 539), and with whom one may be seduced into carrying on that unsatisfactory imitation of an analytic encounter in which the truth of an immediate experience is bypassed.

Perhaps Bion did not complete and publish this paper because it was too close. I think it conceivable that every time he returned to it he risked the breaking through of his own traumatic anxiety and childhood pain. For those who have read his autobiographical writings, his letters to his family, and his war memoir, the personal core of pain in the subject of this paper is palpable in those final four paragraphs, with their Beckett-like metre, and this impression comes out of the blue when it emerges suddenly after the earlier discussions. On close reading, I feel that those earlier passages contain the deeply existential elements of Bion's avowed theme, that of breakage, in various directions, indicating possibilities of injury but also of change and growth.

Notes

1 Bion had written very much along these lines in his 1965 book, *Transformations: Change from Learning to Growth*, when he writes of the resistance to the imminent turbulence felt to issue from transformations which precipitate a shift from T(K → O).

2 "If it seems rather to fall in the column 2 category, it will mean that the statement is known to be false but provides the patient with a theory that will act as a defensive barrier against feelings and ideas that might take its place" (Bion, 1963, *Elements of Psycho-analysis*, Ch. 15).

3 The Long Weekend, Chapter 6.

References

Bion, W. R. (1967). Notes on Memory and Desire. *Psychoanalytic Forum, 2*: 272–723, 279–280. Reprinted in: *Cogitations* (pp. 380–385), ed. F. Bion. London: Karnac, 1994.

Bion, W. R. (1970). Attention and Interpretation: A Scientific Approach to Insight in *Psycho-Analysis and Groups*. London: Karnac Books.

Bion, W. R., (1985). *All My Sins Remembered: Another Part of a Life & The Other Side of Genius: Family Letters*. London: Karnac Books.

Bion Talamo, P. (1981). Ps ⇌ D. *Rivista di Psicoanalisi* 27: 626–628.

Braithwaite, R. B. (1955). *Scientific Explanation*. Cambridge: Cambridge University Press.

Caper, R. (1998). Review of: *The Clinical Thinking of Wilfred Bion*. Symington J., and Symington, N. (1996). *Int. J. Psycho-Anal.*, 79: 417–420.

Freud, S. (1900). *The Interpretation of Dreams. The Standard Edition of the Complete Psychological Works of Sigmund Freud, Volume IV.* London: Penguin Vintage Classics, 2001.

Green, A. (1992). Review of *Cogitations* by Wilfred R. Bion, *Int. J. Psycho-Anal.*, 73: 585–589.

Heisenberg, W. (1958). *Physics and Philosophy: The Revolution in Modern Science*. Lectures delivered at University of St. Andrews, Scotland, Winter 1955–56.

Kavanaugh, K., & Rodriguez, O. (Trans.) (1964). *The Collected Works of St. John of the Cross*. New York: Doubleday.

Keats, J. (1817). Letter to George and Thomas Keats, 21st December 1817, *Letters of John Keats*, Boston: Harvard University Press, 1958.

Solms, M. (1997). *What is Consciousness?;* J. Amer. Psa. Association, 45: 681–778.

Index

For Product Safety Concerns and Information please contact our EU representative GPSR@taylorandfrancis.com
Taylor & Francis Verlag GmbH, Kaufingerstraße 24, 80331 München, Germany

www.ingramcontent.com/pod-product-compliance
Ingram Content Group UK Ltd.
Pitfield, Milton Keynes, MK11 3LW, UK
UKHW020130200926
475702UK00005B/674
* 9 7 8 1 1 3 8 6 1 4 9 9 4 *